"Will You Say a Few Words?"

Also by Jean Carnahan:

If Walls Could Talk:
The Story of Missouri's First Families

Christmas at the Mansion:
Its Memories and Menus

"Will You Say a Few Words?"

Jean Carnahan

2000

To my father,
Reginald A. Carpenter,
who delighted in telling a good story to
anyone who would listen
and to my mother,
Alvina Sullivan Carpenter,
whose impromptu "speeches"
(unappreciated at the time)
helped shaped my life.

Contents

"Tonight is Halloween," Lucy tells Linus.
"How come you're not sitting out in a pumpkin patch
waiting for the Great Pumpkin and making a total,
complete and absolute fool of yourself?"
"You have a nice way of wording things,"
Linus says.
"Thank you," Lucy says.
"I work them out on little slips of paper beforehand."

Introduction

I photographed the figure on the front cover in the Gardens of Versailles. I'm not sure who she is, though the quiver, bow, and animal at her side suggest the Greek goddess Artemis.

Regardless, I was attracted to her heroic posture. I am certain she could champion a cause or overwhelm a mountain lion, if need be.

But could she "say a few words" when called upon?

When people were asked to rank the events they feared most, death came in second to public speaking. (Though I am not sure whether we fear having to deliver a speech or having to endure one—maybe both.)

It has always taken some passion—if not unmitigated gall—to advance ones pet ideas in the public arena. Yet, as First Lady, I feel strongly enough on certain issues to take the risk. Children, the arts, violence, and Missouri heritage have been the focus of my attention during my husband's two terms as governor. This collection of remarks addresses those concerns, though I have also woven in a few of my thoughts on women's issues, literacy, and democracy.

I am often asked if I write my own speeches. Not knowing whether the question suggests a criticism or a compliment, I timidly confess that I have no one to blame but myself.

Most occasions for which I am asked to "say a few words" call for brevity. I try to comply, though it is often tempting to ramble. I generally use notes or a prepared text since my mind is seldom nimble enough for an eloquent, off-the-cuff performance. Nor am I comfortable writing my thoughts on a paper napkin minutes before speaking.

But whatever the length of my talk or the occasion, I try to instill a nugget or two of truth, often wrapped in a story to keep the listeners' attention. I also find that a dash of humor or a heartwarming anecdote make the message—and the messenger—more acceptable to the audience. I hope, however, that the reader will indulge my habit of "cross-pollinating" my speeches, that is, repeating stories or quotations that work well.

I put these "Few Words" into print as evidence that first ladies now voice more opinions then they once did. It's a trend that's likely to continue.

First ladies across the nation are no longer content to host tea parties or to rearrange the furniture in their states' mansions. They are speaking out, cautiously testing their wings.

Their efforts are making a difference on a variety of issues, especially those of primary interest to women, such as child care, breast cancer, and domestic violence.

In her unique position, a First Lady has a perfect platform from which to spotlight neglected issues. Indeed, like the goddess Artemis, she might even lead the charge.

Jean Carnahan
Jefferson City, Missouri
2000

If you have a choice between people giving you wings or people giving you things, make sure you get the wings.
~ Congresswoman Pat Schroeder

Born to Make Barrels
Women Who Put Their Stamp on History

Delivered at the annual Trailblazer's Awards Ceremony, University of Missouri-St. Louis, March 31, 1999, and published in *Vital Speeches of the Day*, June 15, 1999.

I t is good to be on your campus again. I have always been envious of the academic community. I can think of nothing more satisfying than being a perpetual student.

My four children must share some of that feeling, because between them they were able to log in twenty-eight college years.

Having just become a part of the writing community, I've

1

discovered that authors, contrary to popular opinion, actually perform three very useful functions:

They are a godsend to a desperate program chairman needing a speaker.

And they are an absolute necessity for a book signing—though I still remember what happened to the writer, Barbara Bartocci. She said, "I sat for two hours at a book signing table in a department store. During that time three people came by—two of those wanted directions to the rest room."

I have also found that writers provide employment for book reviewers. Having written a hefty volume that weighs over five pounds, I worry that some rougish reviewer might say what John Barrymore once did in a book review. He described a book this way: "It has a *resistible* quality. Once you put it *down*, you can't pick it *up* again."

I enjoyed pondering your topic for the day. When I think of women who have put their stamp on history, I think of so many "Wonder Women" from Lucretia Mott to Eleanor Roosevelt to Sally Ride.

While these names are recognizable to all of us, there are others—teachers, mothers, grandmothers of many here today—who are unsung heroines. They are women who greatly influenced our lives.

But I have also come to admire our 19th-century counterparts—the women who were warriors on the front lines of the slavery, suffrage, and temperance battles.

These early advocates of social justice continue to inspire us today. With few resources at their command, they were forced to use the power of ideas to affect change. The pen became a mighty sword; the voice, a thunderous cannon. They shook the 19th century.

In fact, Nathaniel Hawthorne was so disgusted by the number of female writers that he wrote: "America is now wholly given over to a damned mob of scribbling women."

Today I want to tell you about two of my favorite "scribbling women," because they exemplify some very special traits that we as women have . . .

. . . traits that have served us well over the years,

. . . traits we must not forget we have,

. . . traits that are much needed in the new century.

These two women were 19th-century contemporaries. They were both reared in New England, were married, had large families and overwhelming personal responsibilities. They were especially sensitive to injustice. Both changed the thinking of the nation on the dominant issues of their day—slavery and suffrage.

Beyond that, the similarities cease. One was from a prominent family, the daughter of a renown clergyman. Unlike most women of her time, she was well educated—a teacher and a writer. The other woman was a slave, unable to read or write. But she could speak and she did that quite well.

One was Harriet Beecher Stowe, the author of *Uncle Tom's Cabin*—the woman whose writings did more to arouse the conscience of the nation against slavery than anyone of her day.

The other woman was Isabella Baumfree, who later went by the name Sojourner Truth. She was a remarkable slave woman who stood six feet tall. She had a commanding presence and was one of the early advocates of suffrage and civil rights.

You undoubtedly know something of the accomplishments of these two women. But I doubt if many of you know what they had to overcome day after day to achieve anything.

You may not know that Harriet Beecher Stowe had seven children and a husband who was a hypochondriac. He took to his bed whenever there was a crisis in life, leaving her to manage on her own. Once when the family made a move to another state, Harriet was left to make all the arrangements for moving the household.

In spite of the demands on her, Harriet managed to do what she loved most—to write. At the time, women with political opinions were not taken seriously, but that did not prevent her from expressing her ideas.

She somehow found time to write—letters, articles, entire books—thirty-three literary works in all. *Uncle Tom's Cabin* broke all sales records of its day.

Her success brought her to the attention of the President of the United States. It is said that Abraham Lincoln referred to her as "the little lady whose book started this big war."

But let's go behind the scenes for a minute to see Harriet Beecher Stowe in her other roles. I want to read to you a portion of a letter Stowe wrote to a friend in 1850. Imagine now—she is writing this letter off-and-on throughout the day, whenever she can catch a few moments. Finally, at the close of the day, she sits down at her desk. She dips her pen in ink and by the light of a dimly burning lamp she recounts the day's events to a friend:

I teach an hour a day in our school and I read two hours every day to the children. I am reading Scott's historic novels in their order. I use my leisure hours writing for newspapers. I have written more than anybody, or myself, would have thought.

Yet I am constantly pursued and haunted by the idea that I don't do anything. Since I began this note I have been called off at least a dozen times; once for the fish man to buy a codfish; once to see a man who had brought me a barrel of apples; once to see a man selling books; then next door to Mrs. Upham's to see about a

drawing I promised to make for her; then to nurse the
baby; then into the kitchen to make a chowder for
dinner; and now I am back at my desk again, for
nothing but deadly determination allows me ever to
write; it is rowing against wind and tide.

How familiar this all sounds.

Here is a kindred spirit.

We know exactly what she is talking about. Our interruptions may be different, but the competition for our time sounds all too familiar. Many of you in this room have rowed "against wind and tide" already today or have been doing so for some time.

Harriet recognized what women have known for centuries, that there are duties, intrusions, necessary things that lay claim to our time and thoughts.

Other 19th-century women expressed similar problems. Elizabeth Cady Stanton, for instance, expressed her concern in a letter written to Susan B. Anthony:

"Men who want to work on a document shut themselves away for days with their thoughts and their books. They know little of what difficulties a woman must surmount to get off a tolerable production."

Yes, obstacles and hardships were common denominators in the lives of 19th-century women of achievement.

That was certainly true of Isabella Baumfree. The hearty slave woman faced more than her share of adversity. She was quite a contrast to the very proper, primly dressed, and precisely spoken Mrs. Stowe.

While Harriet Beecher Stowe told a story of a fictional slave family, Isabella's story was very real. She was born a slave in New York state. At the age of eleven, she was separated from her family when she was sold to a new owner.

She eventually wound up working for the extended family—aunts, uncles, cousins—of Mr. and Mrs. John Dumont. Because she was big and strong, the Dumont's required more of Isabella. When she fell in love with a slave on an adjacent farm, Dumont forbade the marriage, and required her to marry one of the older slaves on his own farm.

There is so much legend attached to her story that it's hard to sort out the facts, but we know that she had at least five children. When one of the daughters of the Dumont clan married and moved to Alabama, Mrs. Dumont gave Isabella's five-year-old son to the couple as a wedding gift.

The separation broke Isabella's heart. She came to hate Mrs. Dumont, whom she referred to as the "mean missus."

In time Isabella felt that God was directing her to take her infant daughter and run away. (Though she later said she didn't run away—that would have been illegal—she walked.) She walked to the nearby home of a Quaker couple. They took her in and offered to let her stay for as long as she wanted. In fact, to make the arrangement legal, they bought the remainder of her time as a slave.

Meanwhile, Isabella wanted to retrieve her son. She went back to the Dumonts and pleaded for his return. But the "mean missus" refused. Mrs. Dumont made a statement that, in time, would come back to haunt her. She said to Isabella, "What difference does one little child make to you?"

Isabella got a lawyer and in a landmark decision won the right to have her child returned. When she took him home and removed his clothes, there were large scars across his back from beatings that had been inflicted upon him.

By 1828, New York had abolished slavery. Around the same time, Isabella felt the call to preach. She was 46. She took the name Sojourner Truth because it was her intention to sojourn the land and proclaim the truth.

Since she couldn't read the Bible, Isabella had it read to her, and she memorized large portions of it. She dictated her life's story and sold it to support herself. Wherever she spoke, her simple but dynamic message attracted crowds. While her speeches were unstructured, she confounded the skeptics with plain truth and images from her own life.

But critics hounded her as well. When told that

there were threats to burn the auditorium where she was to speak, Sojourner replied, "Let them burn the building and I will speak upon the ashes."

This next incident in her life seems like it might have been coincidental, but Isabella never thought so. During a visit to the Dumont family, Isabella was there when a letter arrived. The daughter of the family—the one that had married and moved to Alabama—had been brutally murdered by her drunken husband. The "mean missus" was overcome with grief and Isabella remained to care for her.

She later said, "I took the 'mean missus' in my arms, hugged her to my bosom, and rocked her like a little baby."

Isabella understood a mother's grief; she had also come to understand mercy.

I have told you the story of these women today because they point up three traits that have served us well as women.

Women of accomplishment have always been adaptive. They find a way when there is no way. They wear many hats. Being generalists, they come at problems from many different perspectives.

Eleanor Roosevelt once said: "Women have one advantage over men. Throughout history they have been forced to make adjustments. The result is that, in most cases, it is less difficult for a woman to adapt to new situations than it is for a man."

A good example of this can be seen in the life of a St. Louis lady by the name of Frances Gage, or Aunt Fanny as she was known in the women's movement. Aunt Fanny loved to give speeches at the women's conventions. She spoke on the favorite topics of the day—slavery, voting rights, and temperance.

Her speeches weren't just three points and a poem; they were hearty, robust tirades that went on for over an hour, and included an exchange with the audience.

Aunt Fanny often told her audiences about an incident that had inspired her to become an activist on behalf of women. It occurred when she was a young girl growing up on the family farm.

She said: "At age ten, I made my first barrel. It was a beautiful barrel. The cooper who instructed me told my father, 'Fanny made that barrel and has done it quicker and better than any boy I have had after six months training.'"

Fanny beamed with pride as she waited for her fathers approval. Instead he shook his head and replied, "What a pity that you were not born a boy so that you could be good for something. Now, run into the house, child, and go back to your knitting."

She said, "I did knit stockings and my father hired an apprentice boy and paid him two dollars a week to make barrels. Now I was born to make barrels, but they wouldn't let me."

Having been rejected as a barrel maker, Fanny turned her energy to being a speech maker for the women's movement. Her desire to make a perfect barrel transferred to a desire to perfect the rights of women—which brings me to the second trait.

Not only are women adaptive, they are triumphant. Without the traditional power resources—money, position, prestige—they had to rely on their talents and determination.

These women refused to see themselves as too weak, or under-empowered, to make a difference. Their efforts on the critical issues of their time—slavery and suffrage—radically changed the course of the nation.

What would happen today if women pursued such a course with that same vigor?

Today the issue of violence is one that cries out for a woman's touch. Domestic and workplace violence, child abuse, school shootings, road rage, hate crimes, ethnic wars, hate broadcasting, and religious intolerance are shredding the fabric of our society.

What if we as women believed in ourselves again? What if we felt the power to change the future? What if we declared peace and set ourselves upon the task of advancing human rights?

There is one final trait we share with our 19th-century sisters—one that causes me to believe we could make a difference in a violence-proned world. I struggled with finding the right word to describe this trait. I finally came up with the word: genuine.

While these 19th-century women were caring for their families and espousing heroic causes, they were doing something more. They were showing personal compassion and kindness to those who crossed their paths.

They were not just taking political stands—not just writing and speaking about compassion, justice, and mercy. They were engaged in daily acts of human kindness. What they said and what they did matched. What a novel political idea!

Harriet in the midst of her busy day writes, "I must go next door to see Mrs. Upham about a drawing I promised to make for her."

Sojourner recounts, "I held the 'mean missus' in my arms like an infant."

Both their words and deeds illustrated their compassion.

Oliver Goldsmith wrote, "The greatest object in the universe is a good person struggling with adversity—yet there is a still greater one—and that is the good person who comes to relieve it."

The traits of these women are not signs of weakness, but of inner strength—a strength they wanted to share with each other.

These women left their stamp on history with their

ability to be adaptive, triumphant, and genuine. They have also left their stamp on us, their 20th- and 21st-century sisters. For these traits are alive and well in women today.

The ancient poet wrote: "It is the human touch that means more to the aching heart than bread, or shelter, or wine. For shelter is gone when the night is gone, and bread lasts but a day, but the sound of your voice, and the touch of your hand, sings on in the heart always."

In the spirit of these 19th-century women, I urge you to be the voice, the hands, and the heart in this struggle to heal our land and to restore our humanity.

Art sneaks up on you. It teaches you things you didn't know that you needed to. ~ "Peanuts" cartoon character Charlie Brown

The Language of Art

Remarks at the Missouri Arts Awards ceremony of the Missouri Arts Council, Capitol Rotunda, February 6, 1996.

I always look forward to the awards ceremony of the Missouri Arts Council each year. For those of us who spend most of our time in the political world, it is good to be reminded that there is another dimension to life.

I think it's appropriate that we gather in this Capitol Rotunda, surrounded by these wonderful icons of our heritage. They remind us of Missouri's long partnership with the arts.

I just returned last night from the National Governor's Association meeting in Washington. I was thrilled at the chance to see the Vermeer exhibit at the Mellon Art Gallery. The show has had a widespread response. At a White House reception for governors, I mentioned the exhibit when I visited with Mrs. Clinton.

"I don't suppose you've had time to see the Vermeer exhibit?" I asked. She replied that, in fact, both she and the President had made time for a visit to the gallery and had enjoyed it tremendously.

The next day my cab driver—who could barely speak English—showed a similar enthusiasm for the exhibit, as did a waitress later that day.

I realized anew that art is not just for artists. Art is, as Gilbert Chesterton once said, "the signature of the human race." It speaks a universal language.

Next week, here in Jefferson City, we will be receiving an exciting new sculpture. On Valentine's Day, *The Missouri Children's Fountain* will be set on the front lawn of the Governor's Mansion. The fountain has been my dream since 1993 when I learned that there was once a small fountain that sat on the Mansion lawn at the turn of the last century.

It had long been removed, but I found a 1910 picture of the old fountain that showed Governor Hadley's three children playing in the basin. That gave me the idea for erecting a fountain that incorporated the figures of children playing in the falling water. With this concept in mind, the artist, Jamie Anderson, devoted a year to creating a master sculpture.

The classical rendition in bronze depicts three children. The figure on top of the fountain represents Carrie Crittenden, daughter of the 19th-century governor Thomas Crittenden. The nine-year-old girl who died of diphtheria was the only child to die at the Mansion. Her image reminds us of the health needs of our children.

Another figure beneath the flow of the basin depicts an African-American boy reaching into the water. He, too, is a historical figure, described only once by First Lady Agnes Hadley as the "little colored boy who stays in the barn from time to time."

I couldn't get away from that phrase. Why was he there? Had he run away, been abused, or orphaned? We don't know. But today he is shown on the fountain, reminding us that no child should be left out—all should be included.

The third figure depicts today's child. Surrounded by water, birds, fish, and oak and grape leaves, he reminds us to preserve the environment for future generations.

It is my hope that all who see the fountain or live in the Mansion will be reminded of the health, opportunity, and environment of our children.

Yes, the fountain is art with a message. It is a vivid reminder that it is up to those who lead this state to protect the future of Missouri's children. To borrow Chesterton's words again, this fountain could well be the "signature" of this administration and all it holds important.

Again, thank you, Jamie, for creating this timeless sculpture. It is truly an inspired work and a splendid addition to the art treasures of our Capital City.

You must become the change you wish to see in the world.
~ Mohandas Gandhi

The Challenge and the Burden of Leadership

Remarks at the Federation of Women's Democratic Clubs luncheon, Jefferson City, Missouri, October 23, 1993.

When I told Mel I was speaking to you, I said, "I've noticed that when people want a long speech they invite you, but when they want a short one, they ask me."

He said, "Yes, and I notice you're getting more invitations than I am."

I must admit that both Mel and I have been somewhat distracted this week by the birth of our second grandchild. His name is Andrew, he weighs nine pounds, and he's beautiful!

In a real sense, tonight is a celebration for all of us as Democrats. It's been a long time since we've met and had a Democrat in the White House, a Democrat in the Governor's Mansion, and Democrats in most of the statewide offices in Jefferson City.

It's a sweet and long-awaited occasion. Mel and I are grateful for all you did in your communities to make this victory possible.

As I look out on this audience tonight, I see faces of people who have worked actively for our party for a long time—people we can count on in good times and bad.

If there is any secret in politics, it's "don't give up." Keep going. Keep working for the principles and the people you believe in.

Election victories, however, are more than just a cause for celebration, more than just regaining the privileges of office. With victory comes the burden of leadership. It means caring. It means tackling the tough problems, finding answers instead of excuses. Fortunately, Democrats have never shrunk from the responsibility of leadership and we do not today.

We have been living in Jefferson City for nine months now. Still the question I'm asked most frequently is, "How does it feel to live in the Mansion?" Quite truthfully, I'm having the time of my life, working harder than ever.

I remember the first morning after I moved into the Mansion, I went down to the kitchen to get a cup of coffee. I was searching for a cup when one of the prison inmates working at the Mansion came up to me and said, "Mrs. Carnahan, what are you looking for?"

I have to admit that I felt a little intimidated, after all, he had been there longer than I had.

I said, "Oh, I'm just looking for a Styrofoam cup for my coffee."

He was aghast!

He said, "Mrs. Carnahan, the First Lady doesn't drink coffee out of a Styrofoam cup."

I replied, "Oh, please forgive me, I didn't know that!"

Well, I'm learning more and more about the traditions of the house. Hopefully, I won't make another blunder like that. If I do, I'm sure there will be someone to set me straight.

We are the thirtieth family to live in the Mansion. First Lady Jerry Dalton once said, "You can't live here long and not grow to love the house. I always feel I grow a little taller every time I walk through those massive front doors."

I certainly understand what she was talking about. Living in the Mansion is unique because it is both a public building and a private residence. Since the inauguration, over 30,000 people have visited the old Victorian home. We have actually served food to over

7,500 guests. On a few occasions we've had lunches taking place simultaneously on the first and second floors, as well as tours, so it can be a very busy place.

But no matter who visits the Mansion—children or dignitaries, Democrats or Republicans—I want them to enjoy the hospitality of the house. I want our visitors to see the best of Missouri—its products, art work, and musical talent.

Recently, however, I've found that the First Lady does more than serve as hostess and decorator of the Mansion. The destructive floods forced us to put everything aside and concentrate on the incredible misery and destruction Missourians experienced.

But while the flood was devastating to lives and property, it taught us something very valuable. It taught us something about ourselves, as we saw neighbors helping neighbors, and strangers helping strangers. We found strength we didn't know we had.

I found that out when I was working in a Red Cross shelter in Hannibal. I talked to a 79-year-old woman who had no family. She had lost her home and all of her possessions in the flood.

With tears in her eyes, she said, "I even lost my cat." There was no going home for her. Life would never be the same.

As I left, I reached over and took her hand and gave her a hug of encouragement. As we parted, she pulled herself up tall and said something I will never forget. In a spirit that defied defeat, she said, "You know, this old river isn't the only thing that can rise. We can rise above defeat, too."

What a great attitude!

It was the attitude I saw displayed time and again by the flood victims who suffered this tragedy and by the volunteers who came to their rescue.

With the flood behind us, I've turned my attention to some causes of particular concern to me—the health and education of our children.

Children are one of the few groups that cannot lobby for themselves. Labor, business, the elderly—they can speak for themselves. Children cannot. They must rely on others to advocate for them.

On the health side, I've had the opportunity to work on behalf of early childhood immunization. We can now immunize against nine childhood diseases. Yet because of cost, or inconvenience, only 44% of our children under two years of age have all their shots.

Missouri is now making free immunizations available at shopping malls and neighborhood clinics where access is easy. Hopefully, that rate will soon begin to change.* With the help of Hallmark Cards of Kansas City, the Governor and I will be sending congratulatory cards to all new mothers along with an immunization reminder.

* The immunization rate for children under two years of age did increase significantly from 44% in 1993 to 85% by 1999.

Another area related to the health and well-being of children is domestic violence. Our traditional reaction to violence has been somewhat like Mark Twain's reaction to the weather, "Everyone talks about it, but no one does anything." Until recent years, we were not even talking about it.

And yet we know that every 13 seconds a woman is battered somewhere in the United States. We know that six million American women were beaten by the men in their lives. In what sounds like a report on the casualties of war, we know that four thousand were killed, and a million were injured enough to seek medical care last year.

For far too many women and children, home is where the hurt is. While this is not a pleasant matter to discuss, it is one that should be of concern to all women. I hope you will work in your communities to see that women's shelters are built and to do all you can to eradicate this ancient evil.

In the area of education, many of us have been concerned about the lack of support for schools in recent years. That is why the Governor made education the centerpiece of this administration.

Political pundits said it would be nothing short of a miracle if an education reform bill was passed. Well, it did pass. You can be proud of the bold, innovative steps taken by this legislature to give our children new opportunity. I hope you don't forget to thank those Democrats and, yes, those Republicans, who had the courage to put themselves on the line to make it happen because it was the right thing to do.

Back when the legislature was considering the education bill, some reporter commented that the First Lady was seen in the halls of the Capitol. It was thought, he wrote, that she might be doing a "little lobbying" for the education bill.

Well, he was wrong. I "lobbied" shamelessly and without apology for the education bill.

I think that Hillary Clinton, Tipper Gore, and others have set an example for women in politics generally. When we feel strongly on an issue, we should not be silent or intimidated. We should not wait for someone else to right the wrongs in our society. We cannot count on that happening.

Jane Addams certainly didn't wait. Back in the early part of this century, she addressed the needs around her, saying, "If not now, *when*? If not here, *where*? And, if not me, then *who*?"

It is time for Democratic women to seize the moment—our moment. It is time to give our talents to improving our communities.

Whenever we attempt something new, there is always the risk of criticism—the risk of doing something wrong or the risk of failure. Still, we must take the risk of trying.

There is a public expectation that this new Democratic administration in Washington and Jefferson City will take on tough problems, that its leaders will expend the energy needed for accomplishment.

I am proud that Democrats have an optimistic "can do" spirit. Let me tell you a story that tells something about this President and Governor. I was at my desk one evening when Mel came in from the office. He had a stack of papers in his arms that he plopped down on the dining room table.

I said, "We haven't been to a movie for some time. How about going to a show tonight?"

He said, "I'd love to, but just look at this stack of work. Besides that, the President is suppose to call tonight."

So we pushed the papers to one side and ate dinner on the cleared end of the table. After dinner, I went back to work at the computer and he continued working at the dining room table.

By 11:15 p.m., I was still at the computer, but in one of those twilight zones—neither asleep nor fully awake. I was startled when the intercom buzzer sounded. The security officer on the other end said, "Governor, the President is on line one."

Well, I'm still awestruck enough in my new role to get a few goose bumps when the President calls.

Mel picked up the phone and said, "Good evening, Mr. President."

There was a long pause before Mel spoke again.

"That's good news," he said, "I'm glad to hear it." They finished the conversation with some words about the flood and the immediate need for disaster relief in Missouri.

When he was through, I was eager to know why the President had called. Mel explained that a sizable new aircraft contract had just been let that would have a significant impact on Missouri's economy and the President wanted him to know about it in advance of the announcement.

Crawling into bed that night, I thought about the evening and that call. I thought how important it is that we believe in something enough to work for it with all our might for as long as it takes. Adlai Stevenson once said, "What difference does it make if we get elected, or reelected, if we don't stand for something." And, I might add, if we don't work wholeheartedly for something we believe in, or if we don't squander ourselves for a purpose, as John Mason Brown suggested we should.

As Democrats we must be willing to look forward— not just to the next election—but to the next century. Not to look for just the perks of office, but for the possibility to affect change and to find solutions.

Just a few weeks ago we celebrated Columbus Day. We celebrated the life of a man who had the courage to sail off the map. Columbus must surely have been a Democrat at heart to have had that kind of vision.

I hope that when the history of our time is written, it will be said of Democrats that we did not choose the safe harbor.

Rather let it be said that we set sail.

We caught the wind.

We pushed onward through troubled waters.

We found a new way.

That has always been the challenge of the Democratic Party. And today, more than ever, it is OUR challenge.

A hundred years from now it will not matter what my bank account was, the sort of house I lived in, or the kind of car I drove, but the world may be different because I was important in the life of a child. ~ Anonymous

Reflections on Building a "Cathedral"

Remarks at the building dedication, Emergency Children's Care Home (ECHO), St. Louis, Missouri, April 16, 1993.

I saw pictures of your ground breaking last year. Friends of the ECHO children's home had shovels in hand helping to get the building underway.

That picture is worth a thousand words. It showed your work at the ground level. It showed your early commitment to making this project successful. For me to walk in here today and see the outcome of your work is a thrilling experience.

I feel much like I do when I go into a great cathedral. The finished work is magnificent. I am grateful for what has been done. But there is no way to know the vision, the sacrifice, and the work that went into making it possible.

With any project such as this, there are always three groups of people involved. There are those with the dream —the vision of what can be. They have the ideas and are able to inspire others and keep them going.

Then, there are those who make the dream real. They raise the money, they put pencil to paper and mortar to brick.

There are also those who keep the dream alive. They are the staff, volunteers, and supporters who make ECHO work on a day-to-day basis.

You have a long and honorable tradition of service here at ECHO—one that is more than a century old. You know what it takes to keep the dream alive.

However, I've noticed there is a great difference between ECHO and most business enterprises. A typical merchant works as hard as possible to get more business. ECHO works to put itself out of business.

All of us wish that there was no need for ECHO—that you could close the doors. But we know that is not possible. On the contrary, there is a greater demand for your service to youngsters than ever before. According to the

Division of Family Services, reports of abuse and neglect in the City of St. Louis during the month of January alone involved 937 children.

Across the nation, neglect and abuse figures reach 2.5 million. Not only has the reported number of abused and neglected children increased, their problems are more severe and difficult to treat. Abuse is not new, nor is it likely to go away, but I believe we are lowering the tolerance for this kind of behavior.

Nearly two thousand years ago, a "poll" was taken on the road between Jericho and Jerusalem. We are told that only one out of three was willing to turn from their personal pursuits to help someone who had been physically assaulted and left without care.

This story of the Good Samaritan is an ancient and familiar teaching. We are grateful that there are people today who will pause in their own pursuits to help heal the wounds in our society.

When I earlier compared your project to the building of a cathedral, I'm sure many of you thought that was something of an exaggeration. Yet, if I recall my medieval history correctly, a cathedral was built as a place where God was made visible.

Certainly, there is no place where that is truer than in the work you are doing here to provide emergency care for children. You not only give help where it is needed, you give hope when it is lost.

Thank you for letting me share this wonderful day with you. Most of all, thank you for all you are doing for the children who look to you for help.

The only true happiness comes from squandering ourselves for a purpose. ~ John Mason Brown

"Can't You Do Better?"

Speech to the Missouri Baptist Foundation,
Jefferson City, Missouri, November 30, 1993.

Y ou may not agree with this analogy, but I've often thought that people in development work have a lot in common with those of us in politics. Success is closely associated with our ability to convince people to support the causes in which we believe.

We both ask people to do some unusual things. Politicians, for instance, ask people to contribute to their campaign and to break from their routine to go vote. No doubt, you have discovered that it is equally unnatural to expect people to release their money without some tangible, immediate benefit.

Someone has said people think about voting as often as they do the valve stems on their tires. I expect they think about capital causes with even less frequency. Therein lies the challenge.

I recall some years ago being in one of those reflective moods when I was taking stock of myself and the time I was spending in various civic organizations. I discovered that I did not belong to any organization that had more than $37.50 in its treasury.

Don't get me wrong. These organizations had good purposes; their members had good intentions. But they were greatly handicapped by either their inability or reluctance to raise money to accomplish their goals.

Over the years, I've concluded that our mental attitudes toward fund raising greatly affects how successful we will be in achieving our goals.

Now, I don't expect to say anything new tonight—nothing that all of you in this room don't already know. However, as someone once said, we don't go to church to learn anything new; we've heard it all before. We go to remind ourselves of the things we already know to be true. That's what I want to do tonight—just remind all of us of what we know to be true about fund raising.

My comments are based on a conversation that took place in the play *Fiddler on the Roof*—a conversation between a shopkeeper and a street beggar.

The shopkeeper puts a coin in the beggar's cup. The beggar is disgruntled. He reaches into the cup, retrieves the coin, looks up at the shopkeeper and says, "Can't you do better?"

The shopkeeper replies, "I had a bad year."

To which the beggar replies, "Because you had a bad year, I should suffer?"

We in fund raising can relate to the beggar. It puzzles us that people don't see situations or needs as we do. Fortunately, you are not in the business of begging. You are in the business of bringing people and causes together. Let me suggest a few proven ways of doing that.

First of all, you must give potential donors a compelling reason for supporting your cause.

Take Bob, here, for instance. If I want to get $100 from him, how would I go about doing that?

There are number of ways.

I could try fear. I could poke a gun in his ribs. (Many of you may think that's the only way to get Bob to turn loose of his money.)

I could try peer pressure. I could tell him that the rest of you gave me $100.

Or I could write him a letter with a pretty envelope

and his name on the inside. But Bob has seen these things before and chances are he will drop my well-crafted letter into his wastebasket without opening it.

I could try persistence. If I ask Bob often enough for the $100, he'll finally give me $50 just to get rid of me.

I have to give Bob a compelling reason to part with that $100. To do that, I've got to get inside his brain and see what makes him tick. Better yet, I need to know what appeals to his heart.

Earlier this summer, I worked with Missouri Mansion Preservation to get a grant for a three-day statewide children's arts festival. I wanted an event that would bring a variety of art, drama, and music to children from around the state.

I approached the subject with Diane Disney Miller when she was in Missouri to dedicate a sculpture of her late father, Walt Disney. We had lunch together and I explained what I hoped to do. I mentioned that I would like to name the festival after her father, since he lived in Marceline, Missouri, as a boy. She was excited by the idea and indicated that the Disney Foundation might be interested in helping. I should keep in touch, she said.

During the next few days, I hastily put together a proposal and mailed it to her. Some weeks later, I got back a reply. It wasn't what I wanted to hear. The company had given to flood relief and didn't feel they could do any more.

I thought, there's something wrong in this picture. We have given them every reason to accept this proposal. It's an arts festival. It's for children. It's named after Disney who considered Missouri his childhood home.

So I picked up the phone, called Diane Disney Miller, and reviewed the project with her. In doing so, I found they had a problem with making a long-term commitment. When we dealt with those concerns, things began to change. To make a long story short, we got funding for the festival for three years, which was beyond my original expectation.

I learned from that experience that successful fund raising comes when we give people a compelling and irresistible reason to help—one that fits their objectives and not just our own.

Secondly, fund raisers must convey a sense of urgency. Do you know who can give the greatest sense of urgency in fund raising?

It's a teenager.

Watch them in action sometime. He, or she, carefully selects a donor whose capacity is well documented—most generally a close relative. The teenager doesn't care when he asks, what he asks, how much he asks for, or how many times.

The teenager believes that what he wants is the

most important thing in the world. If you give him a minute, he will convince you of the urgency of his cause. I suspect that many of you in this room have responded to such appeals repeatedly. Now, I'm not suggesting we take on the mode of harassment, but there is a need for a burning sense of urgency that comes when we believe in our cause.

Shortly after I made the discovery about the near empty treasuries of all the civic groups I belonged to, I was browsing in a book store. I ran onto a small book in the half-price bin where they had thrown all their books on art.

I had to laugh when I saw this little book entitled *The Art of Fund Raising*. Undoubtedly, some clerk, following instructions, had literally marked down every book related to art.

Thinking it might contain a nugget or two of wisdom, I bought it. Each chapter had a different fund raising technique—some clever, some cutesy. One suggestion was to send a tea bag to potential donors, asking the recipient to invite a friend to tea. Supposedly, the two would discuss the fund raising request and each mail in $10 to the cause.

But it was the last chapter that shocked me. It read, "We've given you lots of ideas for raising money. *Don't use them* unless, for some reason, you can't use the one sure-fired method."

I read on eager to learn the true secret of fund raising. His method seemed so simple that I wondered why I thought it might be a mystery.

The best way to raise funds is to "look your potential donor straight in the eye and ASK! Everything else is a substitute for directly asking."

Well, I have never found a simpler or truer statement about fund raising. Still, we often substitute other methods because we physically can't get around to enough people. But in doing so, we should never forget the best way.

My final suggestion for gaining a donor is to make him, or her, a partner in your cause. It's very important that there be a partnership between the giver and the gift. Donors to church-related colleges, hospitals, and homes for children and the elderly need to feel a link between their gift and God's work on earth.

Someone has said, "The love of God seeps out through our hands—through our pocketbooks—onto the earth." We are not merely receptacles of His blessings, we are conduits—pipelines—for passing on the goodness of God to others. That's what you are each day.

I certainly admire the work you do for future generations through the Missouri Baptist Foundation. I know how hard the task is and how discouraging it can be sometimes.

And yet, we must not settle for being beggars,

pathetically pleading, "Can't you give more?" We are not beggars, but believers that "God's work on earth must truly be our own."

You have been a strength to the needy in . . . distress, a refuge from the storm, a shade from the heat. ~ Isaiah 25:4

Violence is Learned Behavior— But So is Caring

Dedication of the Dr. Barbara Russell Center for victims of domestic violence, Rolla, Missouri, March 13, 1994.

I want to thank you for this opportunity to be here today, to see my home community address an issue of growing concern to all of us.

I am especially pleased that the center we are dedicating today is in memory of Dr. Barbara Russell. She served countless abused women and children during her years of medical practice in this community, so it is fitting that this facility should bear her name.

We're here today to dedicate what is sometimes referred to as a "safe house." That's a strange distinction, isn't it? House and home, by definition, have always been thought to be safe havens, a place where we can be protected against the stresses and strains of life. But, we know that's not always the case.

When I think of our traditional reaction to domestic violence, it has been a lot like Mark Twain's reaction to the weather, "Everyone talks about it, but no one does anything." Until recent years, we were not even talking about it. That's why your being here today is so significant.

Our gathering acknowledges one of society's oldest, most tragic, and most ignored occurances—domestic violence. In recent years, we have come to know more about this hidden menace to women and children.

For instance, we know that last year six million American women were beaten by the men in their lives, four thousand were killed, and a million were injured enough to seek medical care. These figures sound like a report on the casualties of war.

We know that—even as we sit here—every 13 seconds a woman will be battered somewhere in the United States.

We also know that more women—rich and poor—are injured by the men in their lives than by car accidents, muggings, or rape combined.

Yes, for far too many women and children, home is where the hurt is.

But numbers don't tell the whole story. We become desensitized to numbers alone.

Faces tell the story.

Bruised bodies and broken limbs tell the story.

Scarred minds and spirits tell the story.

I grew up in a loving and caring three-generational home. I consider myself one of the most fortunate of children. For many years, I innocently believed all children shared this opportunity. It was a long time before I discovered why my closest childhood friend could spend the night at my house, but for some strange reason—that I couldn't understand—she feared inviting me to her home. And, so I learned about family violence from the whispers of my young friend who was one of its helpless victims.

Today, the good news is there are people in our communities committed to giving women alternatives to abusive relationships. Even so, change has been slow. Those of you on the front lines, tending the wounded victims, know that all too well. No attitudes are more archaic than those related to family violence. We are dealing with generations of old customs deeply embedded in our social and legal structure.

As early as 1800 B.C., the law allowed a man the right to inflict punishment on any member of his household, for after all, they were his property. It was centuries later before British common law provided merciful relief by proscribing that only a stick, no thicker than a man's thumb, could be used to chastise a woman. And so came the expression we still use today, "the rule of thumb."

It was only 100 years ago that a legal opinion on domestic violence in this country stated, "It is better to draw the curtain, shut out the public gaze, and leave the parties to forget and forgive."

That was pretty much our national policy until the 1970s when the curtain was opened revealing the depth of the problem. That year a FBI report disclosed a startling statistic: 12.5% of murders committed in the United States were spouse killings.

Still, we waited until the 1980s before domestic violence was generally considered a crime. Even now, community response is often summed up with such statements as, "It's a private family affair," or "It must be her fault," or "If it's so bad, why does she stay?" Such reactions are all part of our defense mechanism that allows us to look the other way.

It is people like you who will make the difference in public reaction.

It is people like you who will help us focus on the problem and reduce the tolerance we have given to domestic violence.

New behavior can and must be learned. We have learned to be a society intolerant of despotism, slavery, and injustice. We must now become a nation where family violence is inexcusable.

Violence is learned behavior, but so is caring. Both can be taught; both can be transmitted to those around us. Prevention must become the common work of law enforcement, medicine, civic groups, government, schools, churches, and families.

This is not a task for the faint-hearted or the impatient. You will not be greeted with bouquets or ribbons for your efforts. But, I want you to know that the Governor and I are supportive of your efforts on behalf of Missouri families.

It was some years ago that John F. Kennedy reminded us "that God's work must truly be our own." Barbara Russell, who we honor today, understood that well. She exemplified it in her daily work. It is up to each of us to do all we can to remove the ugliness of violence from our communities and to protect those who are victims of abuse. George Washington Carver wrote these lines with which I would like to close:

> How far you go in life
> Depends on your being tender with the young,
> Compassionate with the aged,
> Sympathetic with the striving,
> And tolerant of the weak and the strong.
> Because someday in life
> You will have been all of these.

What we shall need is not geniuses, or cynics, or misanthropes, or clever tacticians, but plain, honest, straight forward men." ~ Diedrich Bonhoffer

"Meet My Husband, the Governor"

Introduction of Governor Mel Carnahan at the Missouri Press Association luncheon, Jefferson City, Missouri, February 12, 1997.

T his is a historic occasion for me. I have never before introduced a governor. Furthermore, I have never introduced my husband. I think he is as nervous as I am about the prospect.

I'll try not to be as wordy as the woman who called the newspaper editor to place her husband's obituary. She gave a long and flowery recitation of her husband's good deeds that she wanted printed in the paper. When she finished, the editor said, "Madam, we have a new policy now. We charge $5 a word."

The woman responded, "Well, in that case just put, 'Sam died.'"

The editor replied, "I'm sorry madam, but there's a five word minimum."

"Oh," she said, "Then put 'Sam died, Cadillac for sale.'"

It's very hard to tell a group of newsmen and women something they don't already know. Those of us in public life are well aware that our lives are an open book, and I accept that. It's part of your duty to see that we are, in fact, what we profess to be.

That leaves me with the task of telling you something about Mel Carnahan that you may not know—things that Chris Sifford has not bothered to reveal in the official one-page bio.

First of all, he's a flying enthusiast and pilot. Mel loves airshows, airplane magazines, anything flight related.

He once worked refueling commercial airplanes. He has flown in a T-6, a DC-3, a F-15, a Harrier jet, and the B-2 simulator. He has flown in a helicopter, a glider, a float plane, and a hot air balloon.

He knows the state, not only from the ground, but from the air as well. I have many times seen him wake up, look out the window of a plane at night, and tell me what city we're flying over. So if someone tells you the Governor's up in the clouds, he may really be.

Mel is pretty much a homebody—as much so as you can be in politics. We get back to our farm in Rolla for some part of most weekends. While we're there, he loves to jump on the tractor and move snow around, or cut brush—whichever is in season.

He also enjoys getting up early and going for a brisk walk in the morning when we're at home. But he has a strange habit; he always carries a bag with him. He comes back with this bag full of cans and debris that he's picked up along our gravel road. I have no doubt that we live on the cleanest road in Phelps County.

Mel not only enjoys the outdoors, he enjoys cooking. He's especially fond of making soup. Pea soup is his specialty, but he makes a great bean soup, too.

The Governor also enjoys singing. He has sung in a church choir for as long as I can remember and for many years in a barbershop quartet. In fact, he helped put himself through law school working as a church choir director.

Today the most I can get out of him is a duet with his brother at the family Thanksgiving gathering. However, I've always felt that his interest in harmony is reflected in his leadership style. He brings people together—tries to get everyone to "sing off the same page," so to speak.

But behind his quiet persona—his Clark Kent exterior—is a man of unusual inner strength, direction, and perseverance.

I discovered that very early when we were both just 15 years old. On our second date, he told me he was going to marry me and run for public office. I laughed. Marriage was the farthest thing from my mind at the time and I knew nothing about politics. But five years later we were walking down the aisle in the same church in which we had met. Five years after that, he was running for his first elective office.

Since then he has been on a city, county, or state ballot 18 times. Two of those times, he suffered devastating defeats.

But his passion for public service never waned. As a youngster, he never wanted to be a fireman, he wanted to be a congressman. His idols were not sports figures, they were political figures—like Adlai Stevenson, Stuart Symington, and Harry Truman.

Today he is doing what he loves most—making government work. He sincerely believes that government can be good and that it can have a positive impact on our lives.

And so, it is with great pride, admiration, and love, that I present to you the best governor in the United States, my husband, Mel Carnahan.

The thing always happens that you believe in; and the belief in a thing makes it happen. ~ Frank Lloyd Wright

"Give Me This Mountain"

Speech delivered at the annual citywide Prayer Breakfast, Springfield, Missouri, May 6, 1993.

I guess by now most of us realize that the world is divided into optimists and pessimists.

I've already observed both here today. The optimists are those of you who think this morning's program is going to be over by eight o'clock.

The pessimists are more like the man who dropped by early and asked for a copy of my speech and said he'd read it in the car.

Several of my favorite optimists are found in the pages of the Old Testament. Now, the word optimist is not used anywhere in the Bible. These unique people are usually described as being men and women of faith or those who believed God.

The incident I want to talk about occurs shortly after the children of Israel leave Egypt and arrive at the edge of the Promised Land.

At this point, they do what any normal group of people would do under the circumstances—they form a committee to see how to proceed. In fact, it is probably the first committee on record. You might enjoy reading about their work in the book of Numbers. You will see that group dynamics have not changed a lot over the centuries.

It is a committee of twelve, selected to represent the makeup of the nation. Their commission is to go into the new land and bring back a report of what they discover.

And that is what they do.

It takes them forty days, so we know it was a thorough investigation. When they come back they are all in agreement. Well . . . somewhat. The land, they agree, is everything that God had promised; it's a land that "flows with milk and honey."

They bring back samples of the produce—grape branches so large they have to be supported on poles carried on the shoulders of the men.

Now that was the good news.

The bad news was that there were giants living in fortified cities. They were people much larger and more powerful than the Israelites.

Ten of the men summed up the majority feeling. They said, "We looked at those giants and we were grasshoppers in their sight. This is too risky. Let's go back to Egypt and forget all about this idea."

Only Joshua and Caleb saw the possibilities.

And so, the tribesmen spent the next forty years wandering around in the wilderness until that generation of pessimists died off.

By the time they stand on the brink of the Jordan River again, they have learned their lesson. They are ready to go in and divide up the land.

At this point, Caleb is 85 years old. You would think that he'd be looking for some fine pasture land on which to retire. Instead, Caleb tells the people that he feels just as good as he did forty years earlier. He has the same enthusiasm, the same optimism.

As the land is being divided, he points to Mount Hebron and says, "Give me this mountain." The rest of the verse goes on to describe the mountain that Caleb asked to receive. It says the Anakims lived there. Yes, those same pesky giants were still there in their stone fortifications.

But here's this 85-year-old optimist still looking for mountains to climb and giants to drive out. And that's exactly what he does.

No wonder the Bible describes him as a man who had a "different spirit"—the spirit of the optimist that has always made the difference in who we are and the way we look at the world.

Some hundreds of years later, another optimist by the name of Jeremiah saw the possibilities rather than the problems.

The city in which he lived was under siege by the King of Babylon. Jeremiah was in jail for giving unpopular political opinions to his own king. He knew his countrymen were about to be swept up and carried off into captivity in a foreign land.

People were in a state of panic. All they could see were the problems—and there were plenty. During this chaotic time, Jeremiah did something that no one else thought about doing.

Do you know what he had the nerve to do?

He bought a piece of real estate!

He bought the land on which the invading army was camped at that very moment!

His reason?

He wrote, "Houses and fields and vineyards will be

possessed in this land again."

What a believer! What an optimist!

We know we cannot always control events, but we can control our reaction to those events. As it's been said, life is 10% what happens to us and 90% how we react to what happens to us.

After this prayer breakfast, most of you will go to your workplaces, or schools, or homes. There are going to be problems waiting there for you, maybe some tough decisions. There are going to be "mountains" in your path. You're going to come face to face with some "giants."

Someone's going to tell you that you're wrong . . . or that you're too old . . . or too young. Someone's going to tell you that these are uncertain times . . . or that what you want to do is too risky . . . or too difficult . . . or that you are in the minority . . . or that what you pro-pose has never been done.

But don't you believe them for a minute!

I love this quotation. I have no idea where it comes from: "I said to the one who stood at the gate of the years, 'Give me a light that I may tread safely into the unknown.' He said, 'No, step out into the darkness and put your hand into the hand of God and it will be far brighter than a light and safer than a known way.'"

Joshua and Caleb and Jeremiah understood this. All optimists understand.

Let me close with this poem that is a favorite of mine because it reflects the spirit of all those who have shown faith and optimism in the face of stern reality.

It is called "Anyway."

People are unreasonable, illogical and self-centered.

LOVE THEM ANYWAY.

If you do good, people will accuse you of selfish, ulterior motives.

DO GOOD ANYWAY.

If you are successful, you will win false friends and true enemies.

SUCCEED ANYWAY.

Honesty and trust make you vulnerable.

BE HONEST AND TRUSTING ANYWAY.

The good you do today will be forgotten tomorrow.

DO GOOD ANYWAY.

The biggest people with the biggest ideas can be shot down by the smallest people with the smallest minds.

THINK BIG ANYWAY.

People favor underdogs, but follow only top dogs.

FIGHT FOR SOME UNDERDOGS ANYWAY.

What you spend years building may be destroyed overnight.

BUILD ANYWAY.

Give the world the best you have and few may ever notice.

BUT GIVE THE WORLD THE BEST YOU HAVE ANYWAY.

External events, colleagues, associates, friends, and hostile
forces will bring enough to cry about. So as often as possible
laugh, and hug somebody. ~ Maya Angelou

Looking on the Bright Side

Welcoming remarks to the Missouri Association Directors of
Volunteer Services, Jefferson City, Missouri, May 27, 1993.

I was enticed to be here today not only because I have known your president for many years, but because of your conference topic, "Humor and Health Care."

Anytime we can inject a dimension of humor into whatever we are doing, whether it's health care or politics, it helps to relieve the tension and to make adjustments easier.

Certainly I have found that true in my own situation. I recently moved from a two-story farmhouse (where I no longer had any children to see after) into a splendid Victorian mansion with a staff of twenty or more to manage.

It took me a while just to find the light switches. During the first week that I was at the Mansion, I went into the kitchen rather timidly to look for a cup of coffee. As you know, the kitchen is staffed by prison inmates. I was looking for a Styrofoam cup, because the wide bowl of the china cups cool the coffee very quickly.

One of the inmates came up to me with a concerned look on his face and said, "Mrs. Carnahan, the First Lady doesn't drink coffee out of a Styrofoam cup."

I said, "Please forgive me, I didn't know that!"

Sensing his concern for propriety and my concern for hot coffee, I told him I would compromise and drink out of a mug—if that was all right with him.

There is no doubt that humor heals, no matter what the occasion. It is especially important for those who deliver and receive health care to look on the bright side.

I remember a book written by Adele Starbird, a long-time columnist for the *St. Louis Post-Dispatch*. In it she tells of visiting her mother in a nursing home. I think the incident shows some humor as well as warmth. The dialogue went like this:

Adele's mother says: "Well, things are going well for me . . . I am on an entirely new track. I'm just trying to be pleasant all the time."

Adele: "Is it a great effort?"

Mother: "Did you ever try it?"

Adele: "No, I'm going to wait until I'm your age before trying anything so drastic."

We both laughed and then she grew serious.

Mother: "It's the only thing that's left now that I can do for anybody. I can't read or write, but I can at least be pleasant and not add to the trouble of others. You know I think that every human being is already carrying about as much as he can bear, and I don't want to make it harder."

"Pleasant?" Adele concludes, "She was more than pleasant—she was GALLANT. She met every crisis in her life with flags flying."

Yes, learning to be pleasant in whatever situation we find ourselves is a challenge for all those who receive and give health care.

Mother Theresa once told a group of volunteers that her purpose had always been to "add quality to life." That's exactly what you do everyday. And that makes you very special people.

Keep smiling!

We shape our buildings; thereafter they shape us.
~ Winston Churchill

If Walls Could Talk

Book review at the Harry S. Truman Library,
Independence, Missouri, March 25, 1999.

I must admit to you that
writing *If Walls Could Talk*
was one of the great pleasures
of my life. I have always enjoyed
writing, even as a child—though
one of my earliest attempts met
with some disapproval.

I recall in grade school that
I composed an amusing little
limerick that I thought worthy
of scratching onto my desk top.
Neither my teacher, nor my

principal, nor my parents felt that my thoughts should be immortalized in such a way. So I learned at a young age that writers must be able to accept rejection.

But even those who use more traditional modes of expression have to deal with those terribly haunting questions: "What made you do it?" "What strange spell were you under when you decided to write a book?"

It's hard to explain, but living at the Governor's Mansion and being caught up in the history and the mystery of the home, it seemed that writing a book was the thing to do.

Tonight I thought I would share with you some of the things I discovered while under the influence of my literary muse.

Fifty governors have served the state—thirty of them lived in the current Mansion. Rather than tell you about any one, I want to share a discovery I made about them in general. Despite the era in which they lived, their politics, and their backgrounds, they were very much alike in a number of ways.

The most apparent similarity is that they were all men.

All were of European descent.

All but one was Protestant.

All but one of the governors who lived in the current Mansion was married. None was divorced at the time he was in office.

All but one governor who lived in this Mansion

survived his term. Interestingly it was the bachelor who didn't survive. I don't know whether there is a correlation there or not.

Most living in this house were country lawyers.

Most were not well-to-do.

Nearly all grew up in small towns.

Only one was born in Kansas City and that was Joe Teasdale. Though some later lived in St. Louis, I could find only one who grew up there.

Most had held some previous public office, although a few of the businessmen leaped in without any earlier experience in government.

Most were Democrats. The Republicans held office in Missouri only after the Civil War, in the 1920s just before the Depression, and again during the Reagan era.

But regardless of their politics, Missouri's governors were fiscal conservatives who followed middle-of-the-road policies. They were not flamboyant in either policy or person.

Also, you might be pleased to know that there was not a scoundrel in the lot—although some were a bit unconventional or given to strong passions.

Governor Stewart, for instance, had a drinking habit that caused him to be viewed as a bit eccentric, especially when he rode his horse into the previous Mansion and fed him oats from the sideboard. But he was, otherwise, a good governor.

There was Claiborne Fox Jackson who ran off with the state seal at the beginning of the Civil War, but passions ran high at the time.

General Phelps got into some hot water when he ran for governor. The 60-year-old Democrat was accused of making sexual advances toward a young woman aboard a steamship. An article about the incident even ran in the *Chicago Tribune*.

It made for spicy reading during the campaign, but nobody believed the esteemed general would do such a thing. In a great show of confidence, they elected him by the largest vote ever given a Missouri governor.

And then there was Governor Gardner—a casket manufacturer—who had shipped bootleg liquor in coffins during Prohibition. But no one took that seriously, except the prohibitionists.

Back in the 1930s, Governor Stark benefited from Tom Pendergast's voting fraud in Kansas City. In one ward, "Boss" Pendergast racked up more votes for the Democrats than there were residents.

One man in charge of altering ballots complained, "Those damn Republicans mark their ballots so hard, they're almost impossible to erase."

Instead of showing gratitude for the extra votes, Stark helped send Pendergast to jail.

So you can see that there were some incidents that raised eyebrows, but as they say in Washington, there was nothing that rose to an impeachable offense.

Along about now you are probably thinking that our state's first families have been boring people. But Missourians like their officials somewhat bland. They don't want too much excitement at the statehouse.

One candidate for the year 2000 was recently described as "plain vanilla." I think that description might serve to his political benefit. Certainly, Missourians would never tolerate California's Jerry Brown or Louisiana's Edmund Edwards. When it comes to politicians, they still prefer the simplicity and straight talk of a Harry Truman.

Well, having explored some of the similarities and idiosyncrasies of our governors, let's look for a while at the other side of the first family equation—the governor's wife. The first ladies also shared some similarities. They all had a job they didn't seek—a job that some even detested.

Serving as First Lady was like being pushed onto the stage without a script. Mrs. Roosevelt was undoubtedly aware of this when she set out her "Seven Practical Rules for First Ladies." Interestingly, two of her rules had to do with riding in the backseat of a car— something she often had to do in an opened-top limousine.

Her first bit of advice was to "lean back in the seat so as not to block the view of your husband."

The other was not to "gain so much weight that you can't sit three to the backseat."

With few rules to guide them, Missouri's gracious first ladies did what was expected of them—for the most part.

And what was expected of them?

One thing.

They were expected to keep the traditions.

What were the traditions?

First, and foremost, was the tradition of hospitality. To neglect the tradition of hospitality was the surest way for a first lady to fall into disfavor in the community and few took that risk.

The hospitable ladies opened the house to one and all. In fact, in the last century, Mansion gatherings were great Jacksonian Democratic events. Everyone in town was invited, including conventioneers and visitors to the city.

Such inclusiveness sometimes led to rowdy events with drinking, pushing, and shoving. Guests often pocketed the food—and sometimes the silver. On at least one occasion, police were stationed at the house to prevent any disorder from occurring.

In addition to these robust gatherings, women of the Capital City expected the first lady to have dainty tea parties, musicals, and formal dinners. Members of the local music club, the DAR, and the War Mothers came to the Mansion regularly.

In keeping with tradition, the First Lady would announce in the paper that she was "at home" to visitors on certain days. Later she returned the visits of her callers. Dressed in her best attire, hat, gloves, and corset, she would get into her buggy and go calling on the other ladies in town. It took stamina to be a Victorian lady; it was not light work.

In addition she had to plan for the traditional entertaining and feeding of the legislature. Lawmakers were invited in groups of 30 to 40 at a time, in alphabetical order. You might find it amusing that we still do that today, because it's convenient. And legislators—because of their schedules—still arrive late and leave early just as they did more than one hundred years ago.

The first lady was also expected to mark the end of her stay at the Mansion with the traditional "change dinner"—a meal given by the outgoing First Family for the new occupants of the house, usually on the day before inauguration.

This worked smoothly when both families were of the same political party. But, as you can imagine, it has not worked too well in recent years when the governors were of opposite parties, or in those cases where they had run against each other.

In addition to extending the hospitality of the Mansion to one and all, the first lady was expected to show compassion for the distressed and afflicted. During wartime, she set an example by wrapping bandages for the Red Cross, selling war bonds, and entertaining soldiers.

During emergencies, she cared for victims of floods, epidemics, and accidents. She showed compassion for prison inmates and their families and often visited the state penitentiary. It was a wretched place—one of the worst in the nation.

Sometimes she went on her own to the prison to visit the female prisoners. But most often, she went with her husband and stood by his side as he delivered a patriotic speech or bestowed holiday pardons.

Her most burdensome task, however, was relieved after the Pardon and Parole Board was established in 1913. Before then, the wife or mother of a prisoner often called on the governor's wife to secure the release of a loved one.

One woman came to the Mansion door, pushed the butler aside, and fell at the feet of the First Lady, pleading for her husband's freedom.

Others threatened to kill themselves on the Mansion steps. It was a terrible burden. One first lady even resorted to using an impersonator to receive those pleading for mercy. But even the impersonator became too stressed for the job.

Well, as you can see, there were many times when

the first lady's compassion and hospitality were greatly tested. But there was another requirement that also tested her endurance. It was expected that the first lady would love and care for the old house. This was something of a challenge, because the house always needed repair.

The roof leaked.

The plumbing was out of sorts.

Rats roamed about the cellar.

Floors were unlevel.

Windows rattled.

The furniture didn't match.

And the soot from trains coated the curtains and furniture.

To make matters worse, the house was built without bathrooms or closets. Until the late 1930s, the first lady was further inconvenienced by having the kitchen located in the damp, dirt-floored basement. It was impossible to get food to the dining room or the third floor at the right temperature.

Despite these inconveniences, the Mansion was never without guests. Its thirteen bedrooms were filled with either friends or kinfolk who moved in to enjoy the benefits of public housing.*

No wonder the first families began complaining about the deteriorating condition of the house just six

---

* During the past 25 years, a large portion of the second floor—originally seven bedrooms—has been converted to the first family private quarters.

years after it was built. Unfortunately, money for repairs was hard to come by. An ongoing struggle developed between first families trying to get comfortable and budget-minded legislators trying to make ends meet.

Some—like the Lloyd Stark family—resolved the situation by paying for many repairs themselves. But when it came time for the major repairs, Mrs. Stark asked the legislature for $50,000. A committee came to inspect the house and found the First Lady in bed with a terrible cold. She had blankets pulled up under her chin and rags stuffed around the windows to keep out the wintry blast.

Well, as they say, one picture is worth a thousand words. In an uncharacteristic display of generosity, the lawmakers gave her $5,000 more than she requested.

Later, during the Donnelly era, the legislators became more intolerant of the old Mansion and its shortcomings. They saw the dilapidated building as a money trap that needed to be demolished.

Lawmakers, eyeing the site for a parking lot, voted funds to construct a nice ranch-style house for the governor across the river. But Donnelly had come to love the old house and vetoed the bill. His decision saved the Mansion for a time when restoration would be more popular than demolition.

Later the Hearnes-Bond restorations, spanning a

decade, gave the house the authentic Victorian style that it has today—a splendor that it deserved, but had never before achieved.

You certainly have to admire an old house that has survived the onslaught of its critics and the good intentions of its many decorators. Today it is one of the finest Victorian restorations in the nation—thanks to the special attention of several recent first ladies.

Missouri's first ladies not only cared for the house and kept the traditions of hospitality and compassion, many of them were doing something more. In what might be called "The Best Kept Secret of the Mansion," many first ladies were giving advice to their husbands, and all the while denying any intrusion in public policy.

Maggie Stephens, for instance, was First Lady before the turn of the 20th century.

She was wealthy and flamboyant.

She gave fabulous parties.

Her gowns were designed after those worn by Marie Antoinette at Versailles.

The Capital City loved Maggie Stephens.

An admirer wrote a poem calling her the Queen of Missouri. (I couldn't resist using that as the title of the Stephens chapter in my book.)

As you might guess, Maggie had lots of opinions and was not afraid to express them. It was said that she lobbied against capital punishment and that she pressured lawmakers to keep the capital in Jefferson City. Her critics also charged that she spent state money for such frivolities as a silver toothpick for the Governor.

But the straw that broke the camel's back came when she talked the Governor into pardoning a St. Louis prostitute who had murdered a state senator following an abusive relationship. It outraged the senators to think that the First Lady would defend someone who had murdered one of their own.

One St. Louis newspaper ran the headline, "Is Missouri Run by a Governess?"

Maggie was mortified at being the subject of a news article. She agreed to talk to the press, but only if her husband was present.

When they gathered, reporters quizzed the First Lady, "Have you lobbied the legislature on the capital punishment bill?"

Now, Maggie was a church-going woman; she was opposed to outright lying, so she was careful how she phrased her responses. Maggie replied that she might have brought up the topic of capital punishment once or twice during a party at the Mansion.

"Did you spend state funds for a silver toothpick?" another reporter asked.

Maggie replied that she would rather not address

such a personal topic.

They asked, "Do you try to influence your husband on legislative matters?"

At that point, Maggie turned on the charm. She fluttered her eyelids and softly replied, "Why, certainly not! I wouldn't think of doing such a thing. He has *by far* the better judgment."

Scarlet O'Hara would have applauded Maggie's performance. Yes, Maggie has been the envy of 20th century first ladies. She got away with more than any governor's wife before, or since, her time.

In my telling of these old anecdotes, I hope you have sensed my fascination with the house and its residents. I discovered what Winston Churchill said to be true, "We shape our buildings; thereafter they shape us."

That is certainly true of those who lived within the walls of the Mansion. I have no doubt that they were the better for having lived there.

It shouldn't hurt to be a child. ~ Slogan of the National
Committee to Prevent Child Abuse

Let Us Remember the Children

Welcoming remarks to the ninth annual meeting of the
Child Care Association, "Have a Heart for Kids Day,"
Capitol Rotunda, Jefferson City, Missouri, February 9, 1993.

I t is a pleasure to welcome
you to the Capitol. When I
told my grown children that I was
going to be with Captain
Kangaroo, they were excited.
After all, he was their first hero.
Believe me, with four children to
care for, he saved my day on
many occasions.

Just last month my husband
said in his inaugural speech
that "children represent only a

small part of our population, but they are 100% of our future."

You are here today to help make that future brighter for more youngsters. You not only give help when it is needed, you give hope where it is lost.

As you begin your session, let me share a few lines from a poem I ran onto recently. I hope you will keep its vivid imagery before you during your meetings today.

Let us remember the children
    who stare at photographers from behind barbed
        wires,
    who can't bound down the streets in a new pair of
        sneakers,
    who never 'counted potatoes,'
    who were born in places where we wouldn't be
        caught dead,
    who never go to the circus,
    who live in an X-rated world.
Let us remember the children
    who never get dessert,
    who have no safe blanket to drag behind them,
    who watch their parents watch them die,
    who can't find any bread to steal,
    who don't have any room to clean up,
    whose pictures aren't on anybody's dresser,
    whose monsters are real.

And let us remember those whose nightmares come true
in the daytime,
who will eat anything,
who have never seen a dentist,
who aren't spoiled by anybody,
who go to bed hungry and cry themselves to sleep.
And let us remember the children who want to be
carried and for those who must,
for those we never give up on and for those who don't
get a second chance,
for those who cling to the shadows and for those who
will grab the hand of anybody kind enough to
offer it.

Thank you again for being a kind hand and heart for Missouri's children. As child care workers and advocates, you are the "still, small voice" of conscience in these legislative halls. When we get bogged down in the day-to-day details of governing, you remind us again to remember the children.

Never let up. You are making a difference in the lives of Missouri's youngest citizens.

We are the great arsenal of democracy. ~ Franklin D. Roosevelt

Freedom is Never Finished

Homecoming welcome to the Missouri National Guard members returning from Bosnia, Jefferson Barracks, St. Louis, Missouri, August 16, 1996.

L ast year before the Christmas trees came down and before the celebration of the New Year began, you had your lives drastically rearranged.

You left your loved ones behind. You put your dreams on hold. You assumed a duty that was important to your nation.

The Governor saw you off, and regrets that he could not be here today for your homecoming.

When you departed for Bosnia, he said that the 1137th was Missouri's best. You have affirmed that and more.

We are proud of what you have done.

We are grateful for your part in this peacekeeping mission.

And, we are proud of the support given you by your families, communities, and employers.

They know—as we all do—that the role of the citizen-soldier is more important today than ever before. Because we live in such a volatile world, we are constantly faced with real or threatened crises. It is only America that has both the strength and the will to be the guardians of world freedom.

Some years ago when President Eisenhower was in the Oval Office, there was a painting hanging on his wall that featured the signing of the Declaration of Independence.

Eisenhower had discovered the art work in the White House storeroom. It was an odd painting to hang because there was a mass of gray, raw canvas around the edge of the picture. The artist had been commissioned by Congress to paint the picture, but died before its completion. Eisenhower had it hung anyway. He said the painting reminded him that freedom is an unfinished work—there is still room for all of us in the picture.

Yes, the work of freedom is never done—not for you,

not for any of us. Here on our shores we need you to help defeat the ancient enemies of our society: intolerance, injustice, and violence. You have seen firsthand what insidious wrongs occur when a country is torn apart by hatreds. We need you to engage in the day-to-day struggle for peace and justice at home just as you have abroad.

The writer Norman Cousins noted that millions of bricks had to be put into place, one by one, over many centuries, in order for us to dwell in the penthouse of freedom.

I first learned that lesson when I was a youngster growing up in Washington, D.C. I often passed the Archives at 7th Street and Pennsylvania Avenue, the building that houses the Declaration of Independence and the Constitution of the United States.

Each time I did, I looked for the words engraved outside that historic building. For a kid, they were big words—words that I could barely pronounce, much less understand. The inscription read, "Eternal Vigilance is the Price of Liberty." Or, as it was later explained to me, freedom is not free, it costs somebody.

This period of your service has been especially costly for most of you. You missed some significant times in the life of your family—births, funerals, graduations, holidays.

When I thought about your sacrifice, I remembered

the words of Thomas Paine during the early days of our nation's history. He said the "summer soldier and the sunshine patriot" would shrink from service when it was inconvenient. Then he went on to add that those who did their duty in times of crisis deserve the love and thanks of every man and woman. And that is what we are here to bestow today.

We are truly grateful for the service that the National Guard has rendered time and again.

Welcome home 1137th and God bless each of you for your service to freedom.

If you want to do something to change the world, you can do that—one child at a time. ~ Clifton David

The Heartbeat and the Drumbeat for Children

Remarks at the Governor's Summit on Early Brain Development, St. Louis, Missouri, November 21, 1997.

When I read who was attending this conference, I was very impressed. I thought of a phrase once used by the writer Christopher Marlowe. He spoke of "infinite riches in a little room." That's what we have here today. Your expertise and your commitment to child care are unique and invaluable. I must admit, however, that I feel somewhat intimidated at the thought of speaking to such a group.

I feel a lot like Charlie Brown did when he, Lucy, and Linus were lying on a hilltop looking overhead at a cloud formation.

Charlie was in a reflective mood, so he asked his friends, "What do you see in those clouds?"

Without hesitation, Lucy replied, "I see the southeast wall of the Sistine Chapel."

Linus said, "I see Raphael's *Madonna*."

Charlie Brown was silent.

"Well, Charlie Brown, what do you see?" Lucy asked.

Charlie replied, "I was going to say a horsy and a piggy, but I don't think I'll bother."

Unlike Charlie Brown and his friends, I believe that all of us at this conference recognize the same thing. The results of new brain research are causes for both alarm and action.

I became aware of how critical this topic is when I was in a department store recently. The clerk had been delayed getting to me because she had been talking very intently to a young lady. She later apologized to me for the wait and went on to tell me about her conversation.

Her friend was about to have a baby. The mother-to-be was very frightened because she had to return to work two weeks after delivery and had found no one to care for the child.

At the time, Louise Woodward was being tried for

the death of an infant in her care. The highly publicized incident was a cause for concern for the young mother-to-be.

She had said to her friend, "I'm worried. Could this happen to my child?" I left the store wondering how many other parents were asking that same question.

Parents today, sitting around their dinner table, are concerned about the quality and cost of child care. They are not thinking about politicians—Newt Gingrich's Contract for America, or Bill Clinton's latest accusation, or Mel Carnahan's legislative agenda.

I might add, they are not thinking about brain research either. They are thinking about paying bills, caring for sick children or aging parents, and keeping their jobs. But all the time, they have this gnawing feeling of guilt about child care.

Many feel their child care arrangement is not what it should be. But either they can't find better—or if they can—it is unaffordable.

Not only are parents concerned about the safety of their children, now we add yet another dimension to that fear. Will brain development be diminished from lack of proper stimulation? There is now the fear of mental neglect, as well as the fear of physical neglect.

That's why those in government and child care work cannot just nod appreciatively at this new brain research. We cannot collect this data, wrap it in an attractive cover, and archive it on a shelf somewhere.

Nor should these discoveries be hidden in academic journals. The findings on early brain development must become the catalyst for action in the child care sector and in government.

Now I am pragmatic enough to know we can't fix the problems of early child care and development all at once. There is no magic wand. But I believe that brain research findings—coupled with the alarm of so many parents—warrant some emergency measures.

Back in World War II, when the nation was beginning to gear up for a full-scale war, we were unable to put state-of-the-art naval vessels into combat. They had not been designed. No one knew exactly what was needed.

But that did not stop the country from proceeding. The Navy built something called Liberty ships—they weren't ideal, but they got us in the water quickly, fighting back. They bought us time to develop what was needed.

Hopefully, the impact of what we are learning and sharing at this conference will impel us to proceed. The alarm has been sounded; it is now time for action.

This fall I had the chance to see the musical *Les Miserables*. As you recall, the main characters in the play care very deeply about the next generation—more than they do their own lives. Because they do, they take some enormous risks, and therein lies the drama and magnetism of the play.

The grand finale features the triumphant song "Do You Hear the People Sing." Part of it goes like this:

> *When the beating of your heart*
> *Echoes the beating of the drums*
> *It is the future that they bring*
> *When tomorrow comes.*

It is you—and people like you—who supply the heartbeat and the drumbeat for children. What we do now will determine tomorrow for all our children.

Life is no brief candle to me. It is sort of a splendid torch which I have got hold of for a moment.
~ George Bernard Shaw

"Please Welcome Barbara Bush"

Introduction of former First Lady Barbara Bush at the "Salute to Literacy," Mexico, Missouri, April 19, 1996.

O ne of my fondest memories as a youngster growing up in Washington D.C. was of the "Book Lady" who came to our school each month.

The "Book Lady" came from the local library. She read poetry and stories that delighted us all. The characters in these books seemed to leap from the page. She made us eager to read. That's the way I would describe our speaker today. She has made America eager to read.

As First Lady, she was expected to promote a favorite cause. But even after she left the White House, she continued to be an advocate for literacy, giving evidence of her abiding devotion to this cause.

She is not only a reader, she is also a writer and has coauthored a book with her dog, Millie. While my dog Beaumont—a 150-pound Newfoundland—can neither read nor write, he can calculate. From any point in the backyard, he can clearly calculate the shortest distance to his food bowl.

There are many tributes we could pay the former First Lady for her warmth and generosity. She truly wrapped her arms around America and we loved it. Six times she was voted the nation's Most Admired Woman.

Her warm smile and gracious manner continue to erase barriers and open doors of understanding wherever she goes.

She conquers every situation with indomitable good humor.

Once when she was asked by a reporter, "Do you see any similarities between you and Hillary Clinton?"

She responded, "Yes, we are both young and good-looking."

We would all agree.

Please welcome Barbara Bush.

Violence is causing the unraveling of the fabric of who we are.
~ News anchor Tom Brokaw

For the Sake of Our Children

Million Mom's Rally against gun violence, April 8, 2000,
Forest Park, St. Louis, Missouri.

Y ou will hear a lot said
about *who* gathered here
today. And, you will hear a lot
said about *why* we are here.

So first, let me clarify
just *who* we are, and *why*
we are here.

We are not a bunch of
gun-hating zealots who
want to take guns away
from responsible, law-abiding
sportsmen.

We are women tired of children killing children.

We are women who are sickened that our kids are being made targets for the reckless and demented who have easy access to guns.

We are women who grieve for the families and friends of the thousands who die from gun injuries each year.

We are women seeking answers, asking why, in one year's time, firearms killed 0 children in Japan, 19 in Great Britain, 57 in Germany, 109 in France, 153 in Canada, but 5,285 in the United States.

We go to bed at night saddened by the dozen children who have died from gunshot wounds that day. For we know that twelve more will die tomorrow, and the next day, and the next, until we, the mothers of America, become angry enough to demand change.

We are women who have instinctively—from the dawn of civilization—rallied to protect our children from harm, and we continue to do so today.

Yes, we are women who love our children.

That is why we are here today.

We want a meaningful handgun policy—one based on common sense, not empty rhetoric. One that puts our children first, not the financial interests of the gun lobby.

We believe that a background check before the purchase of a handgun makes sense.

We believe that selling child-safety locks with new handguns will save lives.

We believe that the strict enforcement of existing laws is essential in curbing handgun deaths.

Millions of moms are asking gun owners and lawmakers to listen to the cries of America's children, and not the tired, old ranting of the past.

I have no doubt that our persistence will make the difference.

Let us not forget that it was women who led the way for every major social reform in America—from slavery, to women's suffrage, to civil rights. Women paraded, and they pleaded, and they prayed until victory was won. We must do no less today.

To the gun lobby, I say, "Do not underestimate our strength. Do not doubt our resolve."

We are calling for meaningful handgun safety legislation by May 14th—Mother's Day 2000. The mothers of America will ultimately achieve this goal for we are committed to saving the lives of our children.

We will not relent.

We will continue to rally across America until our children are safe in their homes, schools, and neighborhoods.

And we will prevail because our cause is right and our hearts are one.

I try to do something good for someone each day without getting caught. ~ A volunteer

Volunteers to the Rescue

Remarks upon receiving the Missouri Citizen of the Year Award from the Missouri March of Dimes, Jefferson City, Missouri, February 25, 1997.

After that splendid introduction, I know how a waffle feels when syrup is poured over it.

What an inspiration it is to be here with Anna Roosevelt and to learn how she is carrying on the work of her grandfather. She not only has the name and warm expression of her grandmother, she also has that same indomitable spirit.

I do want to thank each of you for being here this evening and for

95

this award. It is an evening I will treasure always.

I want most of all to thank you for being here for the March of Dimes.

As a child, I can remember collecting dimes and putting them in a slotted folder for the annual fund-raising drive. In doing so, I felt that I had a small part in helping to eradicate polio that was such a threat to my generation.

It's good to see an organization fulfill its original mission and bravely tackle another, even more complex, challenge, that of birth defects.

Much of the work of the March of Dimes is done by volunteers who give their time and dollars—yes, it takes more than dimes now—to be sure the research continues and treatment is available to all.

I'd like to conclude this wonderful evening with my favorite story about volunteers. It's a salute to you. It tells us something of the spirit and strength of those who willingly share their lives and resources with others.

Back in 1940, the German Army was advancing across Europe, devastating everything in sight. The French Army had collapsed. The Dutch were overwhelmed. The Belgians had surrendered. The British, along with the remains of the French Army, were being chased across France.

The Allied Army finally came to the point where there was no place for them to run. They reached the shoreline of France, a small fishing village called Dunkirk.

Before them was the English Channel some twenty miles across to England. Behind them was the Germany Army that couldn't be stopped. They were literally between the devil and the deep blue sea.

The combined French and British armies amounted to one-third of a million men. Evacuating that many men was impossible because the Germans had bombed the harbor, making it difficult for large troop ships to reach the shore.

The War Office in London met. The military leaders were asked what was the best case scenario. They estimated that they might be able to save 17,000 men. So there was the army—in this apparently hopeless situation—camped along a ten-mile stretch of beach waiting to die.

But early one morning as the troops looked out upon the horizon, they saw something they couldn't believe. It looked like a mirage.

The water was covered with boats!

Fire boats . . . life boats . . . sail boats . . . tug boats . . . yachts . . . ferries . . . anything that could be floated off the shores of England was headed their way.

All were commanded by civilian volunteers.

Those men stranded on the beach at Dunkirk were saved by the small boats that came to their rescue.

Yes, the strength of volunteers is in their numbers.

It is in their readiness to respond.

Fortunately, the spirit of the volunteer is very much alive today.

It is evidenced in the March of Dimes.

It's in this room.

Thank you for this award, but most of all, thank you for coming to the rescue of children with birth defects.

Hold fast to your dreams, for if dreams die, life is a broken-winged bird that cannot fly. ~ African-American poet Langston Hughes

The Power of One

Remarks at the annual birthday celebration of Martin Luther King, Jr. at the Missouri Governor's Mansion, January 13, 1998.

I want to thank each of you for being here tonight to celebrate the life and legacy of Martin Luther King, Jr. All of us take part in these celebrations across our state each year because we have been touched by the life of Dr. King. His dream has become our dream, his mission, our mission.

The life of Martin Luther King, Jr. always reminds me of

the power of one—the possibility that each of us has for righting wrong, no matter who we are or where we are.

When Dr. King began his work, he was not a prominent political figure. He did not have great financial resources at his command. He was a simple Baptist preacher.

He was walking in the footsteps of those who had gone before him. People like Sojourner Truth who embodied the power of one. She was not an attractive media personality; she was a humble slave woman with a commanding presence and a heart-wrenching story.

There was Harriet Beecher Stowe, writer of *Uncle Tom's Cabin*. She was not a social philosopher or a theologian; she was a housewife with seven children.

Rosa Parks was not a revolutionary, she was just a woman who was tired after a day's work and wanted to sit down on a bus.

All of these people appeared so defenseless, insignificant, unknown. Yet they harnessed the inner strength to challenge traditional thinking and to change the course of our nation, not with guns and hatred, but with nonviolence and love.

When Robert Kennedy visited South Africa back in the 1960s, he spoke of the impact each of us can make. He said, "Each time we stand up for an idea, or act to improve the lot of others, or strike out against injustice, we send forth a tiny ripple of hope—and crossing each other from a million different centers of energy and daring—those ripples build a current that can sweep down the mightiest walls of oppression and resistance."

I hope that sometime during this Martin Luther King, Jr. celebration month that you will make some ripples.

I hope that you will stand up for a worthy idea, act to improve the lot of others, or defy injustice.

For we all have some of Martin Luther King, Jr. in us. His work is now our work . . . and there is still much to be done.

How wonderful it is that nobody need wait a single moment before starting to improve the world. ~ Anne Frank

Is There a Future for Women's Organizations?

Keynote address, International P.E.O. Convention, Baltimore, Maryland, September 9, 1999.

Several years ago I was asked to speak to a Business and Professional Women's convention on the topic, "Is there a future for women's organizations?"

In researching the subject, I turned up some information that they probably didn't want to hear. The statistical and demographical evidence was not encouraging.

Consider, for instance, that more women are in the work force than ever before—a trend we are told that is unlikely to change.

In 7 of 10 families, both parents work, and in half of our households there are children under 18 to be cared for.

We are told that 27% of our families are headed by a single mother, placing even more strain on many of today's women.

Furthermore, women remain the primary caregivers in their families. With the increase in longevity, they will have the responsibility for parents for much longer.

Not only do women have added demands placed upon them today, there are more options opened to them. They travel and relocate more frequently. Taking advantage of their increased options, many women have enrolled in adult education classes.

Consider, too, the increased option for their children. There are not just soccer moms, but baseball moms, music moms, ballet moms, and scouting moms. One good thing squeezes out another in the competition for our time and energy.

As I gathered information for my speech, I became more and more perplexed at what I was going to say to these women who had worked so hard to build their organizations.

I was pondering all this as I did my Christmas

shopping. I was standing in a line in a department store waiting to buy a Christmas ornament. Standing behind me was a middle-aged woman who was waiting to buy a similar ornament. We got to talking. She told me she was buying the ornament for a gift exchange at her club.

I said, "What club is that?"

She said, "The Dumpling Club."

I said, "I don't believe I've ever heard of the Dumpling Club."

She said, "Oh, it's one of a kind. We organized it in high school many years ago."

I said, "What do you do?"

She said, "We get together once every two weeks and eat dumplings."

I said, "If I did that, they'd need a wheelbarrow to move me around."

She said, "My dumplings are so light they nearly fly off the plate."

I said, " My mother use to make dumplings like that, but I never learned how."

She said, "Would you like my recipe?"

I said, "Oh, certainly."

Sure enough, a week later this recipe shows up in my mail—dumplings for one hundred people. Unfortunately, I've never found an appropriate group to which I could serve them. Perhaps the legislature.

Why did these women meet week after week to do the same things with the same people? I strongly suspect that something more than eating dumplings was bringing them together. There was apparently a strong bond that had developed over the years, a sense of shared experiences and understanding that fed the spirit.

We may find this account of group behavior amusing until we consider some of our own organizational behavior. We go to church week after week with the same people, to hear the same stories, to perform the same rituals. Why? We go to church, as someone once said, to affirm the things we already know to be true. We do this because the fellowship of believers adds value and meaning to our lives.

Yes, we find solace among friends. Remember last month when we saw those pictures on television following the shooting at the day care center in California? In that haunting scene, the children were not panicked. They were not screaming. They were calmly walking from the building *holding hands*.

Holding hands made them feel secure. It gave them confidence. It was a bond that linked them together. This is true whether we are in a center for children or a home for the aged. We need the strength that we gain from each other.

Yes, women's organizations can survive and flourish in the 21st century, if they add meaning to our lives.

But there is another dimension as well.

I would like to suggest that our survival in the new century will come only if we have both *meaning* and a *mission*.

And what is the mission of P.E.O.? It has never changed. It can be summed up in three words: education of women. We could not have a more noble, more timeless, more necessary cause. Most women will, at some point, live independently—as college students, unmarried working women, divorcees, or widows. For them, education is imperative.

Education today is not like the measles—something we get when we're young so we never have to worry about it again. Women need the benefits of education at every stage of their lives. Single and teenage mothers need an education, immigrant women need to acquire basic employment skills, many divorcees and widows need retraining

P.E.O. has come to the rescue of thousands of women. Since 1907, our Educational Loan Fund has made loans totaling more than $61 million. Our International Peace Scholarship has provided almost $13 million for international women to study in North America. Our Continuing Education Grants have topped the $14 million mark. And Scholar Awards allowing women to work on advanced degrees or research are now near $4 million.

Almost 57,000 women have been the recipients of the projects we support. Nearly 7,000 have graduated from our college at Cottey in my home state. Yes, your generosity and commitment have made a difference in countless lives around the world.

Let me share my own education odyssey with you. I do so knowing that many of you in this room could tell a similar, or more dramatic, story of your own educational pursuits.

One summer when I was ten years old, my mother began working in the government in Washington D.C. It was the patriotic thing to do. World War II was in full sway. It was my responsibility to take care of my grandmother who lived next door and to see that she got to the grocery store. Since she didn't drive, that meant we walked the six blocks to the store each week. I can't tell you how much I disliked this task.

But one day as we arrived at the store, I looked down the street where there was man on a ladder painting a sign on a plate glass window that read "Public Library."

I was so excited! I said, "Granny, is it all right if I go to the new library while you shop? I'll be right there to help with the bags when you get through." Well, she reluctantly agreed.

For the next half hour I thought I was in heaven surrounded by all those wonderful books—more books than I had ever seen in my life.

It seemed like no time before I heard a pecking on the window pane. I looked up and there was my grandmother making beckoning motions for me to come help her with the groceries. I quickly checked out three books and together we wrestled books and bags all the way home.

That week I spent a lot of time on the front porch of our row house, sitting in a squeaky glider as I read my books. During that hot Washington summer, I kept a fly swatter and a glass of Kool-Aid nearby. When I did get up, I can still remember how the glider cushions stuck to my legs. But none of this bothered me because my books had transported me to another world.

By the next week, I was looking forward to our grocery trip. I was still reading one of my books as I walked along the street to the store.

I remember my grandmother saying, "Watch out where you're going, Jean, or you'll trip and fall."

And I said, "Don't worry, Granny, I can read and walk at the same time."

As the summer went on, it troubled me that my grandmother showed no interest in my new found love of reading.

One day I said, "Granny I wish you would read this book. It is really good."

She said no, she wasn't interested.

I said, "But just read this part here, it is so good."

Well, it was then that she told me something I couldn't believe.

She said, "I can't read."

I said, "What do you mean, you can't read? *Everybody* can read."

She told me about growing up on farm down in Virginia. Her mother died and she was the oldest girl living at home. So it fell upon her to care for the house and children. There was never time for school or books. Work and daily survival were more important than reading.

Well, in my youthful exuberance I said, "I'll teach you to read! What do you want to read?"

She said she had always wanted to read the Bible. Well, quite truthfully, at that age that was not my book of choice. But we read the Bible that summer. And I suspect it did me more good than it did her.

My grandmother lived to see me graduate from college. It was a proud moment since I was the first member of my family to attend college. Years later, my mother was equally proud when her granddaughter graduated from the University of Virginia law school.

Just recently when my 9-year-old grandson came to visit me for a week, my daughter flew him to the Capital City to see me. As he emerged from the cockpit, he had on those long, baggy jeans like kids wear today, his shoes were untied, and he was reading a book.

I said, "Be careful, Austin. Watch out where you're walking; you're going to trip and fall."

He said, "Don't worry, Grandma, I can read and walk at the same time."

I said, "I should have known that."

Yes, learning as we go is absolutely essential today. Learning must be an ongoing and never ending part of our lives—a process and not a goal.

That is why the work of P.E.O. in Y2K and beyond is more important than ever.

When we give to the education projects, we have no way of knowing just how profoundly we affect the lives of others. Our lives are interwoven in ways we never dreamed.

The German peasants had a saying, "God gives no linen, but only flax to weave."

Let me give you an example.

Some years ago a member of the English Parliament was journeying in Scotland to make a speech. On his return, his carriage got mired in a muddy ditch along the roadside.

A farm boy with a team of horses happened by and offered to pull him out. It took some time and when it was over, the youngster was a pitiful sight, caked with mud from head to foot.

The gentleman was very appreciative and asked, "How much do I owe you?"

The youngster looked surprised and replied, "Oh, nothing, sir. I'm just glad I was here to help when you needed it."

As they talked, the gentleman learned that the boy wanted to be a doctor. The gentleman thought there was little chance of that happening given the meager circumstances of the youngster. But he gave him his card and said, "If there is ever anything I can do to help, let me know."

Well, that might have been a casual remark for the gentleman, but the boy took it seriously. Some years later, he showed up in London and went to Parliament to look up the gentleman. The guard was reluctant to admit him, but the young man pulled out this mud-smeared card with the name of the lawmaker on it.

The guard took the card to the gentleman. When he looked at the card, he recalled the incident that had taken place some years earlier and called for the young man to come in.

Well, to make a long story short, the boy was still wanting to go to medical school and the gentleman, pleased by the boy's determination, made it possible for him to do so.

Now that's scene one of this story. Let's shift to fifty years later for scene two. Different characters, different location. A prominent world leader is ill with an infection in Morocco while attending a crucial war conference during World War II. He is getting progressively sicker. There is concern for his life. But there is a new drug just being produced called penicillin. It is administered to the world leader and he immediately begins to improve.

Now let's fill in the cast of characters: The drug was discovered by Alexander Fleming, the Scottish boy with the team of horses, and the man who paid for his education was Lord Randolph Churchill, father of the ill statesman, Winston Churchill, who recovered and went on to lead his country to victory.

We never know which act turns the flax into linen.

Recently I met a woman who inquired about my grandchildren. I proudly related some of their recent antics. When I inquired about her grandchildren, she pulled out a picture of her eight-month-old granddaughter—one of the most beautiful little girls I've ever seen.

Tears filled her eyes as she explained that this precious little child was undergoing chemotherapy for a form of pediatric cancer. They don't know what the future holds.

She said, "I have contacted people on the internet all over the world who are praying for my granddaughter."

I squeezed her hand and said, "Add me to that list."

We don't know which prayer turns the flax into linen.

I recall that as a youngster in Sunday School we always put pennies in a can on our birthdays for the number of years we were celebrating. These pennies were going to help the missionaries in China, we were told. I was skeptical; what good were those few pennies? But years later, I visited a church started by missionaries. I met Chinese here in this country who told me of the influence of the missionaries on their lives.

I never knew which penny turned the flax into linen.

When you return home, I want you to take the mission of P.E.O. more seriously. Talk to a student or prospective student about education. Talk to a relative, a neighbor, a friend. Encourage them. And if you feel so inclined, help them financially. For next to love, education is the most powerful and lasting gift we can give another.

P.E.O.s can be justly proud of their historic values and steadfast vision.

But a new century calls for new resolve.

In this, our last convention of the 20th century, let us reaffirm the virtues upon which P.E.O. was founded.

Let us take up the cause of educating women with a new passion.

And may the objects and aims of our sisterhood continue to guide us in all the duties of life.

Many things can wait, the child cannot. Now is the time his bones are being formed, his blood is being made, his mind is being developed. To him we cannot say tomorrow, his name is today. ~ Chilean poet Gabriela Mistral

Wake Up to Child Care

Speaking on tour in 1999 for the Child Care at Work initiative.

If Rip Van Winkle were to wake up after being asleep for twenty or thirty years, he would be amazed by a number of things.

His wife has probably replaced his favorite casserole—the one laced with sour cream—with some healthier, trendier dish.

His home would, no doubt, be filled with new electronic gadgets, from computers to

VCRs to digital cameras. Perhaps most exciting of all, his stock portfolio would have quadrupled in value.

But Rip would also notice a change in his family. His wife, in all likelihood, has a job, joining the other 53 million women now in the workplace.

His daughter might be a single parent faced with the problems of finding affordable, quality child care.

Mr. Van Winkle would also find that our views on child care have changed, largely because of what we now know about early brain development.

It was once believed that if a child was diapered and fed regularly, there was little else of significance to be accomplished during those early years.

Now we know better.

Recent brain studies have proven that those early influences matter more than we ever imagined.

When a father comforts a crying newborn, or a mother plays peekaboo with a 10-month old, or a child care worker reads to a toddler, thousands of brain cells respond.

Synaptic connections are strengthened and others are formed. The network grows daily from a handful of pathways at birth to trillions of connections by age three. Such simple activities as holding, rocking, talking, reading, and touching affect how the brain is wired. When these new experiences fail to occur, fewer connections form, and some are pruned away from nonuse.

Yes, the interaction between a child and an adult does make a difference. The architecture of the brain is dramatically impacted by what goes on during the first three years of life. A child's formal education may not start until kindergarten, but we know that learning begins in the crib.

Knowing this presents us with both good news and bad news.

The bad news is that far too many of our children are in mediocre day care settings. Many spend as much as 35 hours a week in substandard care. We see the results later when one in three children arrives in kindergarten unprepared to learn.

While some mothers are able to care for their children at home during this critical period, others must work to make ends meet.

One in four children lives in a single-parent home with only one provider. Over 60% of homes with children have two working parents. For most of these families, day care is a primary concern and cost.

The good news is that more people recognize that these first years count.

Parents, providers, and politicians are beginning to recognize that child care is more than babysitting; it is early childhood education.

Employers, too, recognize that they benefit when workers feel secure about child care arrangements.

When workers know that their children are safe and well cared for, absenteeism and turnover go down. Morale and productivity improve.

The founder of Young Entrepreneurs Network said in the *Kansas City Star* last week, "Many young leaders in business are searching for what's right for the family, what's right for the employee, as well as for what's right for the bottom line."

This new attitude is a contrast to how many employers felt at the turn of the last century. Children worked in sweat shops, coal mines, and factories. Poor children were tools of production and little thought was given to their education.

Today we recognize that the well-being of our economy rests on the strength of all our families. Some companies even provide scholarships and loans to their employees to benefit family education.

Some, like our speaker today, have been at the forefront of workplace child care. Fred Epstein, owner of INDEECO, a manufacturer of electric heating equipment and controls, started an on-site day care center in 1985 at his St. Louis plant. Today he has a well-trained, professional staff offering quality care for more than 100 children ages two to five years old.

Fred and I have spoken to Chambers of Commerce, civic clubs, and company executives all over the state about the benefits of on-site, or near-site, day care.

One of my favorite stories points up the mutuality of interests between workers and employers in respect to child care. It's a true story about three 12-year-old youngsters competing in a 500-meter race in the Special Olympics in Colorado.

Before the race, each of their coaches gave them a pep talk, telling them not to stop for anything or to get diverted from their goal.

"Just run straight for the finish line as fast as you can," they told the physically handicapped youngsters.

The boys did just that. But within yards of the finish line, one of them stumbled and fell.

The other two stopped dead in their tracks. They turned back, helped their friend to his feet, dusted him off, and together they ran hand in hand to the goal line for a three-way tie.

We all benefit by working hand in hand to help each other achieve our goals as employers, families, and communities. Yes, quality child care can be a win for all of us. What you once thought was out of the question for your business, might now be a viable option in a collaborative effort with other employers.

I urge you to take a good look at the child care needs of those in your work force. For as the writer Gabriela Mistral reminds us, "Many things can wait, the child cannot . . . . To him we cannot say tomorrow, his name is today."

There is always one moment in childhood when the door opens and lets the future in. ~ Graham Greene

Hope in Hopeless Times

Professional Development Institute Banquet,
St. Louis, Missouri, October 7, 1999.

T hank you for this opportunity to be with you tonight. I am told that during World War I, it was the custom to take the military leaders who were comfortably seated behind their desks in the War Department and send them onto the battlefield where they could see, and feel, and hear the real battle.

As foot soldiers in the battle to save our children, you are part of a great crusade, as worthy as any ever waged. There is much to be learned from you.

In my efforts to be where the action is, I have had
some wonderful experiences. I recently visited a
Caring Communities site in an area where more than
50% of the children live below the poverty level. As you
know, Caring Communities was set up by an executive
order of the Governor during his first year in office. It's
a new concept in delivering family services. Schools
become "one-stop shops"— the hub of the community
for delivering health services, adult literacy classes,
and after-school tutoring.

I have also been working with officers of the National
Guard and the D.A.R.E. program to take a drug-free
message to students around the state.

My husband also enjoys getting out of the Capital
City. He is especially pleased to see Missouri's education dollars at work in the classrooms—to see the
results of programs he set in place. It is particularly
gratifying to him to visit a school that has made significant strides in student achievement.

There are, indeed, many rewards to public service—
some of which are unexpected. Last year, for instance,
I was reading to children and their parents at a library
during literacy week. When I finished, I was told that
one of the youngsters wanted to present me with a gift.

As I looked up the aisle, there was a little boy
headed toward me. The news media gathered around to

get a picture of the presentation. The youngster was holding a deep, aluminum foil pan with a raised see-through cover like you might get at a bakery.

I thought to myself, "Isn't this sweet. His mother has baked me a cake to show their appreciation for my coming here today."

Well, when he got to me, I reached out to take the cake. As I did, I looked right at the little boy and said, "Oh, thank you so much, I know the Governor and I will enjoy eating . . ."

Just then, I looked down.

It was not a cake at all!

It was a pan full of locust shells! His prize collection. Hundreds and hundreds of locust shells that he had collected over the summer.

Well, my eyes popped! My jaw dropped! The cameras flashed.

I didn't know what to say.

Finally, I recovered enough to mutter, "I believe this is the most unique and memorable gift I have ever received."

The next day my picture was on the front page of the newspaper in color. The photographer—having captured the moment—titled the picture with just one word, "Yuk!"

As we all know, children can make us laugh and they can make us cry. They can lift our spirits and they can sadden our hearts.

I often ask teachers or youth workers what differences do they see in children today. I know I've asked your director that question. He told me that the problems today are much more deeply rooted, more difficult to address.

I asked a school bus driver—the one who drove all of our children to school, the one I had to account to for my children's behavior from time to time. She said, "Kids today are more verbally abusive to each other."

I posed the same question to a classroom teacher of some thirty years. She observed that parents seemed less interested and that home stresses were greater.

Those of you working on the front lines know this to be true. But the most disturbing change of events is the increase in physical violence.

Far too many children are exposed to violence in the home and community every day. They witness everything from verbal and physical abuse to homicides. If learning comes from repetition and example, then society is teaching violence well.

Sadly, far too many are becoming desensitized to violence. But there are people like you who are concerned and that's why you have taken time for this weekend seminar.

You are looking for ways to identify those who are potential victims of violence and to make appropriate interventions.

We know there are factors that predispose families to violent reactions. Let me mention a few on which there is general agreement:

1. High levels of stress within the family caused by financial, marital, or health problems over extended periods.

2. Substance abuse.

3. Social isolation that occurs from an absence of strong ties with family, neighbors, or church; a feeling of being cut off, of being alone in a hostile environment.

4. A history of family violence that comes from poor coping skills and poor problem-solving ability.

5. Certain inherited traits that play a part in putting a child at risk—impulsiveness, fearlessness, learning difficulties.

6. Simply being a male, expected to be rough and tough, adds to the risk of violent behavior.

When we see any of these conditions in a family, it should send out flashing lights to those in education and social services.

The American Psychiatric Association's Commission on Violence and Youth came to a conclusion that is worth noting. They found that an eight-year-old's school behavior predicted how aggressive he would be as a teenager and adult. Altering behavior after age eight is possible, but much more difficult and the chance of success diminished.

Based on these findings, the commission went on to stress the importance of early intervention. While the average age for a juvenile crime is 14.5 years of age, there are warning signals much earlier. Patterns of behavior that include defiance, verbal assaults, and lying emerge much earlier.

Identifying the at-risk child and early intervention are key parts of any effort to prevent violence. This is the role that many of you have. You could certainly give specific ways in which intervention has been appropriate and helpful.

Let's look briefly at a few interventions that have been successful.

The formation of a trusting bond with a nurturing adult outside the family is frequently effective. The at-risk child is often faced with moral confusion, stemming from conduct of parents, leaders, and athletes. Cultural messages received from TV, movies, and pop music add to the confusion. You may well be the only anchor for a child who is desperately in need of a positive role model and a different perspective on life.

The teaching of stress management, problem solving, and anger control is another positive intervention.

Intervention is also a powerful deterrent. Studies show that when there is a collective willingness of adults to intervene when kids misbehave, there is less juvenile crime in a neighborhood.

Informal monitoring is also effective. Where there is a network that keeps parents informed when a kid skips school, or acts disrespectfully, or writes graffiti on a wall, neighborhoods are safer.

I grew up in Washington D.C. in a neighborhood not too unlike some in St. Louis City. There were blocks and blocks of row houses—hundreds of them and they all looked alike.

Each street was named for a letter of the alphabet. We lived on "S" Street. I first learned the alphabet— not to be able to read—but just to find my way home.

But if I misbehaved, no matter whether it was on "S" Street, or "T" Street, or "U" Street, word had already reach my house before I arrived. My mother was waiting there with her arms crossed, wanting an explanation of my conduct.

I recall that years later, we all marveled when some scientist invented an early warning system to alert everyone quickly to any threat to our communities. Well, I have to tell you, they were not the first. The mothers on "S" Street invented that back in the 1940s.

Another intervention is the reinforcement of self-esteem that comes by teaching hobbies, skills, or creative pursuits. It's been said that a child who picks up a violin is not likely to pick up a gun; one who picks up a paint brush is not likely to pick up a needle.

But the title of your seminar, "Hope in Hopeless Times," suggests the most important thing you do for children. You offer hope. Each of you is in the business of exporting hope. You deliver hope and help to those who don't know where to turn.

One of my favorite theologians was Dr. Elton Trueblood. He was once asked how he wanted to be remembered. After all, he was a great preacher, a superb writer, and a teacher. He replied that he wanted to be remembered as an encourager.

That's your role—and it's mine, too. And, sometimes we succeed and sometimes we don't.

But when I go to worrying about the success of my efforts, I always remember what Mother Theresa once said. Someone asked her, "Why do you keep on with your work of caring for the dying and the most destitute of people. It's all so futile. It's all so hopeless."

She replied, "Oh, I am not called to succeed. I am called to be true to my mission." She was one of those who saw things that were hopeless and yet determined to make them otherwise.

It has been said that each of us comes to earth with "sealed orders." It is our duty to open and respond to those orders.

I suspect that part of your "sealed orders" has to do with children—children who are adrift in a sea of moral confusion, needing physical and spiritual care. I commend you for responding each day to that duty. I believe your commitment to the needs of children puts you among those of whom Oliver Goldsmith once wrote. He said, "The greatest object in the universe is a good person struggling with adversity, yet there is a still greater one and that is the good person that comes to relieve it."

Thank you for all the unrecognized things you do each day for children. And thank you for bringing hope and help to Missouri's youngest citizens.

The habit of reading is a man's bulwark against loneliness, his window opening on life, his unending delight.
~ Eleanor Roosevelt

Libraries: Then and Now

Keynote address, Missouri State Librarians' Convention, St. Louis, Missouri, October 14, 1999.

In the process of writing two books, I have developed a new appreciation for libraries and for those who keep and catalog information.

I found a wealth of information at my fingertips in nearby libraries—information, like pieces of a jigsaw puzzle, waiting to be put together in whatever way excited my imagination.

My assistant would call me sometimes at the end of the day

with some tidbit of information she had uncovered—
something that plugged a hole in our research. We
were so excited! You would think we were a couple of
scientists discovering a new planet. Frankly, I miss the
research and the thrill of discovery it brought.

Having published two books, I've discovered that
authors perform several useful functions in society
beyond their writing. They are a godsend to a
desperate program chairman needing a speaker.

Besides that, writers are an absolute necessity at a
book signing—though I still remember what happened
to the writer, Barbara Bartocci.

She said, "I sat for two hours at a book signing table in
a department store. During that time, three people came
by—two of those wanted directions to the rest room."

Writers also provide employment for book reviewers. My first book—a hefty volume that weights more
than five pounds—caused me to worry that some
rougish reviewer might say what John Barrymore once
did in a book review. He described a book this way, "It
has a *resistible* quality. Once you put it *down*, you can't
pick it *up* again."

One of my favorite people served as our local
librarian for many years. Some of you who have been
around for a while may remember Leola Millar, the
grandmother of Melissa Carr, one of your association
members.

Leola wore hats with an air of great confidence that convinced you she knew exactly who she was and what she was about.

She spoke with animation and intensity, even in the hallowed reading room.

She told stories to kids, cooked gourmet dishes, and voted Republican—except when she found an occasional Democrat who met her expectations.

She was so unlike the first librarian in my life—a frumpy, high school librarian by the name of Miss Mowbry. Our paths crossed at a time when I needed one more credit hour and the only thing available was library science.

Well, back in the 1950s this was not considered a cool course—largely because of Miss Mowbry. She was a stereotype figure, with her hair pulled back in a tight bun in which she inserted a pencil.

She always wore gym shoes, at a time when they were only worn for sports. The library books, she said, were her children. She talked to them and handled them gently.

Hanging in her office were the words from a 12th-century English manuscript—a special curse muttered against those who mutilated books or absconded with them:

"This book belongs to St. Mary of Robert's Bridge and whosoever shall steal it, or sell it, or in any way alienate it from this house or mutilate it . . . let him be forever accursed. Amen."

How would you like to post that in your library?

Well, it was in this environment that I began my stint as a librarian assistant. It was my job to collect overdue fines from my fellow students—an unpleasant task that certainly didn't endear me to my classmates.

Miss Mowbry also required me to learn the Dewey decimal system, which I thought was about as useful as learning Morse code. When I advanced suitably, she entrusted me with lettering the numbers on the spine of the books.

Though I didn't admit it to anyone, I came to look forward to my hour with Miss Mowbry, despite her quaint habits.

I even grew to love her "children," though I never learned to talk to them.

So, if I were going to dedicate these remarks to anyone, it would have to be to dear Miss Mowbry. For wherever she might be, she certainly would be shocked—or at least quietly amused—at my being here tonight.

I warn you, though, that I am not a public speaker; I am a storyteller. I find that taking a nugget or two of truth and wrapping it in a story makes both the message and the messenger more tolerable.

However, I could not be here tonight without sharing a very personal story of how a local library profoundly influenced my life.

One summer when I was ten years old, my mother began working in the government in Washington D.C. It was the patriotic thing to do. World War II was in full sway.

It was my responsibility to take care of my grandmother who lived next door and to see that she got to the grocery store.

Since she didn't drive, that meant we walked the six blocks to the store each week. I can't tell you just how much I disliked that task. But one day as we arrived at the store, I looked down the street where there was a man on a ladder painting on the plate glass window the words "Public Library."

I was so excited! I said, "Granny, is it all right if I go to the new library while you shop? I'll be right there to help with the bags when you get through."

Well, she reluctantly agreed. For the next half hour I thought I was in heaven surrounded by all those wonderful books—more books than I had ever seen in my life.

It seemed like no time before I heard a pecking on the window pane. I looked up and there was my grandmother making beckoning motions for me to come help her with the groceries.

I quickly checked out three books and we juggled books and bags all the way home.

I spent the next week reading my books every

chance I got. It was a hot, humid summer, as I recall, so I spent much of the time on the front porch of our row house. Sitting there in the squeaky glider with a fly swatter and a glass of Kool-Aid nearby, I was in another world.

By the next week, I had finished my books, and was looking forward to the grocery shopping trip and my chance to get more books at the library.

As time went on, however, it troubled me that my grandmother showed no interest in my new found love of reading.

One day I said,"Granny, I wish you would read this book. It is really good."

She said no, she wasn't interested.

I said, "But just read this part here, it is so good."

Well, it was then that she told me something I couldn't believe.

She said, "I can't read."

I said, "What do you mean, you can't read? *Everybody* can read!"

She told me about growing up on a farm in Virginia. When her mother died, she was the oldest girl living at home, so it fell upon her to care for the house and the children. There was never time for school or books. Work and daily survival were more important than reading.

Well, in my youthful exuberance I said, "I'll teach

you to read! What do you want to read?"

She said she had always wanted to read the Bible. Well, quite truthfully, at that time that was not my book of choice. But we read the Bible that summer and I suspect it did me more good than it did her.

I thought of that very special summer when I was reading to my grandsons recently. We were reading *Winnie the Pooh*. In the story, Pooh—who loves to eat—goes down into the hole to visit the rabbit and indulges in so much honey and milk that he becomes too large to squeeze back out.

Realizing that he is stuck in this hole until he loses weight, Pooh says to Christopher Robin, "Would you read a sustaining book, such as would help and comfort a wedged bear in great tightness?"

"A sustaining book."

I love that phrase.

Some books are like that. They feed the soul . . . sweep the cobwebs from our minds . . . expand our horizons.

Books can sustain us in so many ways as we thirst for knowledge, or inspiration, or hunger for companionship.

Remember the movie *Shadowlands*?

It's the story of the writer C. S. Lewis. In one scene, he poses a question to one of his Oxford students who has a great love for books.

He asks, "Why do we read?"

The student gives an interesting reply. He answers, "We read to know we're not alone."

He expressed what readers over the centuries have discovered. Reading introduces us to people and ideas—past and present—that we might not otherwise know. Plato awaits us at our public library, as does Aristotle and Spinoza. Keats, Shelly, and Dickinson are waiting there to share their thoughts with us.

We are not alone.

Books that we read and reread tell us something about who we are. I have kept some books by my bedside for years, not because I haven't read them, but because I enjoy rereading them.

One of those books is by Adele Chomeau Starbird who wrote a column for the *St. Louis Post-Dispatch* for decades. I never met her, but I consider her an old friend.

I like her spunky attitude about life. She shows a high regard for such timeless, but oft forgotten qualities such as duty, gallantry, and civility.

She was a member of what E. M. Forster called that "band of old aristocrats," which he described when he wrote:

"I believe in aristocracy. Not an aristocracy of power, based on rank and influence, but an aristocracy of the sensitive, the considerate, and the plucky. Its members are to be found in all nations and classes and through

*the ages, and there is a secret understanding between
them when they meet. They represent the true human
condition and a permanent victory of mankind over
cruelty and chaos."*

Yet, in spite of the wondrous power of words to
transform and to lift us—as the writings of Mrs. Starbird
and others do—there are still many who choose to
remain alone.

We are told that 60% of all adult Americans have
never read a book from cover to cover and most of the
others read only one book a year.

On the other hand, there are those who feel lonely
without books—like St. Jerome—who advised his
followers to keep a "book always in your hand or under
your eyes."

I am one of those who is magnetically drawn to
musty, old bookstores. I love the ruffle of pages
between my fingers. I count those hours best spent
when I can snuggle up beside the fireplace with a good
book.

Each time I try to fit another book onto the shelves
of my home, however, I think of the story of the 10th-
century Persian sheik who had a library made up of
117,000 scrolls. He was a traveling merchant who did
not want to be without his books, so he loaded them
onto four hundred camels and trained them to walk in
alphabetical order.

The story reminds us that libraries must be adaptive to the needs of people. Libraries must fit the way people live and study and work.

Today's library is not just a row of neatly cataloged books as it was in Miss Mowbry's day, or when Melissa's grandmother served as our local librarian.

Today libraries no longer hold just bound information, but boundless knowledge. As we move into a new century, community library services will not diminish. Instead, they will evolve in astonishing new ways yet undreamed.

I envy you.

How exciting it is to be an integral part of the information age.

But whether we read for information or pure pleasure, I believe John Cole of the Library of Congress had it right. I will close with his observation.

He said, "Reading is a joy not dulled by age; a polite and unpunishable vice, a serene and lifelong intoxication."

And so it is.

I find the important thing in the world is not so much where we stand, as in what direction we are moving.
~ Justice Oliver Wendall Holmes

A Proud Heritage

Keynote address to the Missouri Federation of Women's Democratic Clubs annual convention, Springfield, Missouri, October 23, 1999.

T he first time I came to Springfield to a political gathering, I met Billie Babb. It was Jackson Day, 1980.

Mel had been out of political office for 14 years, practicing law and working for other state and national candidates.

But in 1980, he was back in the arena, running for state treasurer. We knew very few people and most did not know us.

141

Billie—and others of you in this room—took us in. You gave us advice and encouragement. Mel and I have never forgotten that.

On our way home after Jackson Day, we wrote down the names of all the people that we could remember. It was just a small stack of 3x5 cards, but it was the beginning of our computerized database of thousands of supporters today.

Billie, you and our other friends in Springfield were in that very first—and very small—card file. You have been special friends ever since. Having received so many solicitation letters from us over the years, by now you may be asking, "How do I get *off* that list?"

Over the last seven years as First Lady, I have had some wonderful experiences and opportunities that I would never have had otherwise.

Just a few months ago, for instance, I went to Iowa to help First Lady Christy Vilsack work on a Habitat for Humanity building project.

I worked alongside the African-American couple who would soon be first-time home owners. I got a little sunburn and some sore thumbs, but it was a very rewarding experience.

Currently I am working to get employers to establish more on-site day care facilities in Missouri. With more parents working outside the home, there is an increased need for quality, affordable day care.

But never let it be said that those of us in politics don't get our just reward. For instance, this year at the State Fair when they had the pig races, one of those cute, little porkers was named for me—Jean Carna-HAM. In one of her races, Carna-HAM was a winner by a snout, having nosed out another runner known as SWILL-ary Rod-HAM Clinton. It was a wonderful honor.

Mel and I also get to showcase our state to visitors. Two months ago, Missouri hosted the National Governors' Association in St. Louis. One of the places we took the first ladies was to an inner-city school. It's a model of what is being done in computer education to reach at-risk children—those children who have already been identified as potential dropouts because of certain risk factors.

The teacher was very excited as she told us about the computer-centered teaching of these youngsters. She said that the absentee rate had dropped and student achievement levels improved. She explained that the kids want to come to school early and to stay after class to work on the computers.

A group of these at-risk fourth graders returned to school before it opened, just to demonstrate how they use the computer as a learning tool.

When it was my turn to go into the computer lab, I sat next to youngster who had a sheet of paper with a number of questions on it that he was to answer by using the computer.

As I sat down I said, "What are you studying?"

He said, "Entomology."

Before I could ask "What's that?" he explained that it was the study of insects.

He said, "Do you know what the heaviest insect in the world is?"

Before I could guess, he replied, "It's the African Goliath beetle. It weighs the same as a quarter pounder."

I said, "I didn't know that, but I'll certainly remember it the next time I'm at McDonalds."

He pulled up the picture of another insect on the screen and said, "This is a black widow spider. It has eight eyes."

Well, I didn't know that either.

He said, "Do you know what color an insect's blood is?"

Somehow I knew it wasn't going to be red. I said "Purple?"

He pointed to the screen and said, "No, yellow or green."

Well, by this time I had learned all I wanted to know about bugs.

I said, "Can you find out who the Governor is?"

He looked at me somewhat puzzled and said, "I already know who the Governor is."

So I pushed him one step farther. I said, "Do you know who the First Lady is?"

He said, "No, but I can find out for you."

He did a few things on the computer and up came a picture of me and Mel. He looked at the picture for a moment, then he looked over at me and back at the screen again, and said, "Is that your little sister?"

I said, "No, that's me on a good day."

I tell you this story to let you know that we are going to hold on to these kids. We are going to save them from dropping out of school or doing drugs. We're going to give them a chance to be productive, useful citizens.

To do that depends not only on those computers and those excited teachers, it depends a lot on whom you elect to office.

That's why this election 2000 is so important. We're talking about the future. We're talking about the lives of young people.

During the darkest days of World War II, Thornton Wilder wrote a Pulitzer prize-winning play entitled *The Skin of our Teeth*. In the play, mankind is represented by George Antrobus and his family—a prehistoric family facing the threat of an Ice Age glacier.

Antrobus, the hero of the play, cautions his family repeatedly, saying, "Don't let the fire go out."

At one point, he makes a heroic statement—one that is a good reminder for us as Democrats standing on the brink of a new century.

He declares, "I know that every good and excellent thing in the world stands moment by moment on the razor-edge of danger and must be fought for, whether it's a field, or a home, or a country."

Democrats are fighting for those things that are in danger today. Democrats in Washington are struggling to save Social Security, to strengthen Medicare, to pay down the national debt, to provide a patients' bill of rights, and to give targeted tax cuts that don't harm services to the neediest in our society.

These are the things Democrats stand for today. They have always stood up for hard-working, middle-class families. I know they did for my family.

I was born during the heart of the Depression. My mother and father both had jobs—they were the lucky ones. Together they brought home about $30 a week.

To make ends meet, they lived with several other family members and shared expenses. Together, they held on during those lean years, often gathering around the radio to listen to the words of hope that came from President Franklin Roosevelt.

By the time I was five years old, the country was coming out of the Depression, largely because of the programs put into place by President Roosevelt.

It was then that my parents bought their first house. Neither one of them had ever owned a home before, nor had their parents. The American dream had not reached us yet.

It was a row house. Every one looked like the other—hundreds of them—with a front porch, and a fenced backyard, and three small bedrooms. I remember the huge billboard posted on the vacant lot across the street. It read, "New FHA Homes for Sale, $5,990. No Money Down. Government Guaranteed Loans."

My parents bought one of those houses and I grew up in it. I walked to the public school several blocks away and went to the Baptist church that stood on the corner.

Those three things—home, school, and church—were the foundation of that neighborhood.

My parents paid into Social Security, confident that it would be there when they needed it because Mr. Roosevelt said that it would.

When the young men in our neighborhood returned from World War II, many of them went to school on the GI Bill. It was a postwar program that opened up a whole new world for those young people.

Even now, when I attend a college graduation, I get misty-eyed—the way some people do at weddings—because I see the American dream coming true for those graduates and their families. You can pick them out. For some, it's the first time anyone in the family has ever graduated from college and many have done so because of student loans.

Yes, Democrats should be proud of their heritage—proud of who we are and what we have done to deliver the American dream.

The Democratic Party gave hope and opportunity to my family. They continue to give hope and opportunity to hard-working families today.

Sometimes we forget who our real constituency is as Democrats. If you ever forget, look back at the 1948 presidential campaign.

The Republican-dominated Congress refused to pass an education bill, refused to halt inflation and run away prices, refused to build low-cost housing, and refused to pass civil rights legislation.

They removed 750,000 people from Social Security over Truman's veto.

They even fought against moving the minimum wage to 75 cents an hour, saying that to do so would expand government and increase taxes.

Does any of this sound familiar?

Harry Truman called them a "do nothing" Congress and the term stuck.

Still things looked pretty bleak for the man who had replaced President Roosevelt and was attempting to run for the office in his own right. One writer referred to Truman as a "puny figure compared to FDR."

When Truman stood before the Democratic

Convention that year, he said something that a lot of those delegates didn't really believe in their hearts. But Harry believed it and he said what he felt.

He said, "We will win this election because they are wrong and we are right. We will win this election because we are the people's party and they are the party of special interests. It's always been that way and it always will be."

Truman said, "If farmers don't give the Democratic Party their support, they will be the most ungrateful people on the face of the earth."

"Labor has never had but one friend in politics," he told his audience, "and that's the Democratic Party."

Still Democrats were disheartened.

Everything pointed to defeat.

The party was divided. Strom Thurman had bolted the convention to form the Dixiecrat Party. In the north, liberal Democrats lined up with Henry Wallace to form the Progressive Party.

But Harry knew who made up the real constituency of the Democratic Party. He got on a train during the final months of the campaign and traveled over 30,000 miles, delivering 271 speeches in 36 states.

In Chicago, 5,000 met him at the train and 100,000 cheered along his parade route. In Boston, a quarter million people came out to hear him.

Still, the news media was unconvinced. They had it

figured out. Harry was a loser. One writer labeled Truman "a game little fellow who went down fighting with all he had." The Republican nominee, Governor Thomas E. Dewey of New York, was a shoe in according to the pollster Thomas Roper. His organization stopped polling in early September, saying Dewey was as good as elected. There was no more need to poll.

Life magazine blatantly referred to Dewey as the next president. And, of course, you remember the headlines in the *Chicago Tribune.*

On the weekend before the election, Truman ended his whistlestop campaign in St. Louis. He spoke to 50,000 people standing in a drizzling rain.

On Sunday at Kiel Auditorium, he spoke to 12,000. The ear-splitting ovation could be heard by the 10,000 who stood outside.

He told his audience that he had the Republicans on the run. This time they believed him.

Standing on stage with his father, the congressman, was a boy who was greatly influenced by the message he heard that evening. The youngster was Mel Carnahan who would later take on a number of tough battles on his way to the governorship.

He learned a valuable lesson from Harry—as we all did. For on election day, Truman confounded the experts and embarrassed the pollsters when he carried 28 states to Dewey's 16, winning by two million more votes than Governor Dewey.

Today when the Republicans are once again ready to anoint their favorite for the presidency, let us remember the lessons of 1948.

Let us remember who our constituency is.

Let us remember the power of grassroots work.

And let us remember who we are.

We are the party that dreams, and dares, and delivers.

We want no part of cynicism, or skepticism, or negativism, or extremism.

We are Democrats.

Martin Luther King, Jr. once said, "You ought to believe something in life, believe that thing so fervently that you will stand up with it till the end of your days."

That's how I feel about the Democratic Party. I believe that's the way you feel, too.

Don't let the fire go out.

In a society where the rights and potential of women are constrained, no man can be truly free. He may have power, but he will not have freedom. ~ Mary Robinson

A New Cloak of Freedom

ERA Rally, Missouri State Capitol, Jefferson City, Missouri, December 1, 1999.

T he Biblical writer gives some timely advice, well suited for today's gathering.

He wrote, "Wherefore seeing we are compassed about with so great a cloud of witnesses . . . let us run with patience the race that is set before us."

Standing beneath this majestic Capitol dome, it is not hard to imagine that we are "compassed about" by those

153

spirits of the past who championed the cause of freedom, equality, and justice.

Many of them did not live to see their dreams come true. But the spirit of those early patriots is very much alive here today—from Lucretia Mott to Rosa Parks, from Susan B. Anthony to Sue Shear.

Your being here—the heirs of these brave souls—is a tribute to their work and to your own resolve.

I have always thought it ironic that the first women's rights convention was spawned at a tea party in upstate New York, seventy years after a tea party for freedom was held in Boston Harbor.

In some instances, the grievances of those women who gathered at the Seneca Falls Convention in 1848 were similar to those of their colonial forefathers.

Women had no voice in the formation of the laws under which they lived.

Nor did they have property rights, voting rights, or the right to hold office.

Most occupations were closed to them and, when they did work, it was for far less than men earned.

They had little access to higher education and none at all to the legal or medical professions.

My maternal ancestors in this country go back into 17th-century Virginia. My great-grandmother was born in the same county as George Washington and James Madison—but the similarities end there.

She had little schooling, never traveled beyond the next town, never held property, never earned any money of her own, never spoke or held an office in her parish church, never cast a vote.

The wife of a Scotch-Irish tenant farmer, she bore seven children and went to an early grave.

I doubt if she ever heard of the Seneca Falls Convention or Elizabeth Cady Stanton. But her granddaughters and great-granddaughters were the beneficiaries of their brave deeds.

Today we are asking the Missouri legislature, and ultimately our nation, to emblazon into the Constitution the simple premise—long overdue—that "equality of rights under the law shall not be denied or abridged on account of sex."

Let us weave these words into a new cloak of freedom, one large enough to cover every man and woman in America.

For the sake of our forebearers, for ourselves, and for the women of the 21st century, let us make the Equal Rights Amendment a constitutional right.

Let equality of opportunity be the mission of this new era, not for ourselves alone, but for women around the globe—women who labor for substandard wages, or are subject to degrading and restrictive laws, or are denied education or birth control information.

For we are still the standard bearers for women in

the worldwide struggle for economic and social justice. Our victories bring them hope.

But as Elizabeth Cady Stanton reminded the women at the Seneca Fall Convention, in doing "the great work before us, we can anticipate misconception, misrepresentation, and ridicule." Her words were, indeed, prophetic.

But whatever the cost, let us determine to hold fast to freedom, knowing that it is our task to pass it on to our children like a priceless heirloom—a treasure for all time and for all people.

Nothing that is done for children is ever wasted.
~ Anonymous

Wishes Can Come True

Dedication of the Stonegate Elementary School,
Raymore, Missouri, February 22, 2000.

T hank you for inviting me to be with you for the dedication of this fine new school. I have had a chance to tour the building and meet some of your teachers and administrators. I am very impressed.

I couldn't help but notice how much your school differs from the grade school that I attended, or even from the one that my children attended. And it is drastically different from one-room schools my parents attended at the beginning of the last century.

Some years ago, my husband and I went to an auction of a one-room schoolhouse and its contents. The building had been abandoned and boarded up for years and it was about to be torn down.

As I recall, we came home from the auction with three items that day: a small desk—for $1; an old fly-specked portrait of George Washington that had hung on the school wall for who knows how long—for 50 cents; and, the bargain of the day, an upright piano with a slightly cracked sound board and several missing ivories—for $3.

By our standards today, those one-room schools were pretty bleak. Typically, there were rows of homemade desks and benches, a wood stove, and a chalk board. Portraits of the presidents usually hung on the wall, along with a world map and a chart of the alphabet.

The library was little more than a shelf of well-worn books, usually supplied by the teacher.

Paper was scarce. Students wrote their lessons upon a stone slate and erased their marks with a piece of sheepskin attached to a block of wood.

In those days, physical education was called recess. The playground equipment was seldom more than a wooden swing under a shade tree, a bat and ball, or a set of monkey bars. And, of course, there was the essential outhouse located at the back of the school yard and a bell perched on the school roof to summon the students.

Students walked to school—often barefooted. Those without shoes did not attend during the bad winter months.

School boards hired the best teachers they could afford, given the economic situation of the community. Generally, the schoolmarm's or schoolmasters had little preparation for teaching. They were quite young, often near the age of their older pupils. Still, teachers were always held in high regard in the community. Local families gave them food and other necessities, and even invited them to dinner from time to time.

Well, before you start yearning for the fringe benefits of those good-old days, we might note some of the hardships of being a pupil or teacher in a one-room school. It was a time when special needs children or gifted children had to adjust to the one-size-fits-all system.

Teaching had some unusual requirements, too. The teacher was expected to arrive at school early enough to draw the water from the well, to have the fire lit to warm the building, and to raise the flag on the school yard. After school, the teacher performed the janitorial duties and, at least once a week, scrubbed the wood floor.

Some teacher contracts even regulated social life, requiring the schoolmarm to be at home by 8 p.m., unless the school board gave permission for later hours. Teachers had no benefits, sick leave, or vacations. When the teacher was sick, school was closed.

We need only look around us to see what dramatic changes this past century has made in public education. Now schools are racing to keep up with the growing technology of a new century. The challenge of teaching and learning is greater than it has ever been before. There are more academic demands on both teachers and students.

Let me give you a graphic example of the growth in knowledge. We are told that from the time of Christ until about the time of the American Revolution (some 1700 years), knowledge doubled. One-hundred and fifty years later, it doubled again, and then again in only fifty years. Today knowledge doubles every four or five years.

Educating a child today is more complex than it has ever been in the history of mankind. Expectations are higher and competition is keener.

What does all this mean for Stonegate School? A school that is determined to keep pace in today's world. You already have a facility and faculty that is second to none. But there is even more that I would wish for you as we dedicate this building tonight.

Let's suppose that I have a magic lantern here tonight. I rubbed it and out jumps a wonderful genie who says, "You have one wish. I will grant you anything you want for Stonegate School." What should I say? What would you say? What would we wish for Stonegate that would be of lasting value?

After thinking about this for some time, I finally decided on my wish: I would ask that Stonegate School always be an exciting place to learn . . . that children would get up in the morning eager to attend because wonderful things are happening here and they don't want to miss anything.

I had some of those feelings last month when I attended the Super Bowl in Atlanta. Now you talk about excitement! The teams, the coaches, the fans were fired up. The Rams and the Titans players were prepared to give their very best to this game. Their coaches had spent long hours teaching the proper techniques needed to move the ball. The stadium overflowed with loyal supporters, wearing the colors and cheering their team onward.

As I looked back on that experience, I thought, "If we can have that kind of enthusiasm for a football team, how much more supportive should we be of our public schools?"

We need parents and the community to be cheerleaders for our schools. We need teachers who can coach students to perform at their best. We need students who show up, prepared and ready to tackle anything before them.

Yes, football is an exciting game and its records are filed away in the annals of sports history. But education is even more exciting, because it is shaping minds and opening doors for our young people every day.

It is wonderful to see a community recognize the value of its schools. Let me close with this one final story. One of the things the Governor enjoys most as he travels around the state is visiting schools. He always comes home thrilled about the great things that are happening in our schools. The Outstanding Schools Act that was passed during his first term in office has laid the foundation for major improvements in education here in Missouri.

One school he visited recently is located at Malta Bend, a small community near Marshall, Missouri. There are only two hundred students in their entire school system. In the early 1990s, Malta Bend was about to lose it accreditation because of poor academic performance.

The community decided it didn't want that to happen. They took advantage of the incentives and enrichment made possible through the Outstanding Schools Act. They passed a school levy to make needed improvements. The local American Legion and the auxiliary came in and did some of the needed repairs and others pitched in to help. Today that school is not only accredited, it is accredited *with distinction*—the best designation possible under the school improvement program.

The dropout rate is 1.9% and the attendance rate is 98%. Things like that don't happen by accident. It's the result of a team effort in that community. Malta Bend has gone from a failing performance to a first-class performance because that community got enthusiastic about its schools.

Whether it's Malta Bend or Stonegate Elementary, we know that our wishes will not be granted magically by some good-natured genie.

The real magic for Stonegate is in this room. Students, teachers, administrators, parents, community members—you are the magic!

It is you, and you alone, who will make Stonegate an exciting place to learn. And, in doing so, you will prepare Stonegate students for whatever they choose in life.

Peace has its victories, but it takes brave men and women to win them. ~ Ralph Waldo Emerson

Partners in Peace

Fort Leonard Wood's U.S. Army Road March and Salute to Veterans, State Capitol steps, Jefferson City, Missouri, March 11, 2000.

T he last time an army near this size marched into Jefferson City was back in 1861.

It was the Union Army under the command of General Nathaniel Lyon. He and his 2,500 men sailed up the Missouri River and took the capital without firing a shot.

The Governor, Claiborne Fox Jackson, was not at all pleased

to see them. In fact, he fled to Boonville to join the opposing army.

While Governor Carnahan is unable to be here to welcome you today, I can assure you that *he is pleased* to be "invaded" by the fine troops from Fort Leonard Wood. In fact, he marched with you during a similar event earlier this year.

I think the timing of this march is appropriate. In a few weeks it will be Memorial Day. We will be honoring the heroic men and women who gave their lives for our country.

Here today, on the steps of our Capitol, however, I think it is fitting that we honor all those who devote themselves to the cause of freedom—especially those who are stationed in our state. You march in the footsteps of others who have bravely fought our nation's battles.

I recently talked to a World War II veteran who went back to visit some of the towns and villages in France that he had helped to liberate on V-E Day.

This time he was walking with a cane in his hand rather than a rifle on his shoulder.

He wore a small lapel insignia of his old combat unit. It was a copy of the cloth badge that he had worn on his arm when he marched across France over fifty years earlier.

One day during his visit, he came face to face with an old woman as he walked along the streets of a village.

She put out her hand to stop him for a moment as she pointed to his lapel pin.

With tears in her eyes, she threw her arms around the old soldier, and in words he couldn't understand, she poured out her heart in gratitude.

As a child, she had seen that insignia when he, along with hundreds of other American soldiers, had marched into her town.

It was a symbol of freedom and deliverance that she had never forgotten through the years.

As members of today's U.S. Army, you continue to be the guardians of world freedom. You are truly peacemakers in a volatile and uncertain world—a world where we are constantly faced with real or threatened crises.

I hope this march today will be a symbol of your renewed commitment to fight the ancient enemies of mankind: injustice, intolerance, and violence.

Our nation needs all of us—military and civilian—to engage in the day-to-day struggle for peace at home and abroad.

To be effective, we must become partners—as we have been today—marching shoulder to shoulder to keep our country strong.

Thanks to each of you for participating in this march.

Thank you, too, for guarding our nation, for in doing so, you insure the well-being of all of America's communities.

Far away in the sunshine are my highest aspirations. I may not reach them, but I can look up and see the beauty, believe in them and follow where they lead. ~ Louisa May Alcott

Hold on to Your Dreams

Keynote address to the Zonta Club's Women of Achievement luncheon, Jefferson City, Missouri, May 16, 2000.

W hen I think of the abundant talent and abilities gathered within the confines of this room, I know what the writer Christopher Marlowe must have had in mind when he used the expression "infinite riches in a little room."

Jefferson City has been richly blessed by the contributions you have made over the years. You in this room have blessed our community beyond measure. I want to thank the Zonta Club for recognizing your many accomplishments.

I want to thank you, too, for this wonderful honor you have bestowed upon me with the "Celebration of Children Award."

I must tell you, though, that this recognition pales in comparison to one I received a few years ago at the State Fair. As you know, they have pig races each year. One of those cute, little piglets was named for me— "Jean Carna-HAM." In one of her races, Carna-HAM was a winner by a snout, having nosed out another contestant named "SWILL-ary Rod-HAM Clinton."

It was a splendid moment.

In preparing to speak to you today, I first considered taking a speech out of the file that I had given before. I thought I could polish it up a bit and it would work just fine. But as I thought about it more, I decided to talk to you about something that is more personal—a topic on which most of us can relate in some way.

Let me begin by telling you about an incident that took place years ago when I was interviewing a young man for a job. He was in his early 40s and quite pleasant. We had lunch and shared some things about his qualifications and background.

Then I looked him in the eye and asked, "What do you want to be when you grow up?"

He looked a little startled by the question. But then

a smile came over his face and he said, "Oh, I know what you're getting at. You want to know if I still have any dreams."

That was exactly what I was aiming for. You see, if I know something about your dreams, I have a pretty good idea of what motivates you. I have a better idea of who you really are.

If I were to ask a group such as this, "How many of you still have some dreams?" most of you would raise your hand.

But if I asked you to share those dreams with the person next to you, or even with your family, many of you would say, "No, I can't do that."

The problem with dreams is that they are often very personal. They are often misunderstood. Someone might laugh.

I grew up in a house of dreams.

It was not a dream house, by any means. My parents had survived the Great Depression, but not without some permanent scars that affected the way they lived and how they looked at the world.

Their dream was to own their own home. And although I was only five years old at the time, I can still remember what an important step that first purchase was. It was a row house in a new subdivision, just like the other three hundred that were built at the time.

But it was a dream come true for them.

I remember their thrill in furnishing our home, piece by piece. My mother crocheted doilies for the tables and chair backs and stitched quilts and afghans for the bedrooms.

My parents grew flowers and vegetables in the back yard each summer. I remember my father building a rose trellis and a back porch, and finishing off the basement.

He even helped our neighbors with their building projects.

I watched dreams come true.

As a youngster, I took all that for granted. I had a different set of dreams. I enjoyed reading. I spent a lot of time sitting on the squeaky glider on the front porch with a glass of Kool-Aid in one hand and a book in the other.

As I read, I became fascinated by the magic of words and convinced that I wanted to be a writer—maybe a reporter or a novelist.

But when I shared my dream with my family and friends, I found no one was as excited about the prospect as I was. In fact, my mother warned me that anyone who followed such a course was likely to have a scant livelihood.

When I went to college—in one of my few concessions to practicality—I majored in Business

Administration. But for my electives, I chose philoso-
phy, literature, history, and writing—things that
stirred my soul.

When I got ready to get married, I found that my
husband-to-be held some dreams of his own—dreams
that I didn't understand.

When my mother heard that Mel intended to devote
his life to public service, she let it be know that, in her
view, politics was a highly unreliable line of work with
few financial benefits.

As it turned out, she was exactly right.

Well, in the ensuing years, I felt a lot like Erma
Bombeck did back in the 50s as a suburban mom. She
wrote, "I hid my dreams in the back of my mind—it
was the only safe place in the house. From time to
time, I would get them out and play with them, not
daring to reveal them to anyone else because they were
fragile and might get broken."

But in the early 1960s, she began writing from her
home and went on to be a highly successful writer. For
Mel and me, it was not until the 1990s that our dreams
converged when we moved into the Governor's
Mansion, giving us the chance to fulfill some long-held
aspirations.

While we were nurturing our own dreams, it
became apparent that our children were working on
their own dreams. It is such a temptation to tell our

children what they should do, or not do, with their lives. So I try to restrain myself.

One of our children wants to rebuild the inner city. He lives in a warehouse in downtown St. Louis. He calls it a loft apartment. It's a matter of perspective. I told him, "If that's what you want to do, go to it."

Another wanted to run the New York marathon. I said, "Fine, give it your best shot."

Another wanted to climb mountains in Tibet and New Guinea. I said, "If you must do it, wear warm socks."

One of the great things about Zonta Club is that you are not only working on your own dreams, you are helping others make their dreams come true.

That is one of life's greatest joys.

When we help others succeed, we unleash a power that has potential for changing the course of events beyond anything we can imagine.

Let me give you an example.

Some years ago a member of the English Parliament was traveling in Scotland to make a speech. On his return, his carriage got mired in a muddy ditch along the roadside.

A farm boy with a team of horses happened by and offered to pull him out. It took some time and when it was over the youngster was a pitiful sight, caked with mud from head to foot.

The gentleman was very appreciative and asked, "How much do I owe you?"

The youngster looked surprised and replied, "Oh, nothing, sir. I'm just glad I was here to help when you needed it."

As they talked, the gentleman learned that the boy wanted to be a doctor. The gentleman thought there was little chance of that happening, given the meager circumstances of the youngster. But he gave him his card and said, "If there is ever anything I can do to help, let me know."

Well, that might have been a casual remark for the gentleman, but the boy took it seriously. Some years later, he showed up in London and went to Parliament to look up the gentleman. The guard was reluctant to admit him, but the young man pulled out this mud-smeared card with the name of the lawmaker on it.

The guard took the card to the lawmaker. When he looked at the card, he recalled the incident that had taken place some years earlier and called for the young man to come in.

Well, to make a long story short, the boy was still wanting to go to medical school and the gentleman, pleased by the boy's determination, made it possible for him to do so.

Now that's scene one of this story. Let's shift to fifty years later for scene two—different characters, different location.

A prominent world leader is ill with an infection in Morocco while attending a crucial war conference during World War II. He is getting progressively sicker. There is concern for his life. But there is a new drug just being produced called penicillin. It is administered to the world leader and he immediately begins to improve.

Now let's fill in the cast of characters.

The drug was discovered by Alexander Fleming, the Scottish boy with the team of horses. The man who paid for his education was Lord Randolph Churchill, father of the ill statesman, Winston Churchill, who recovered and went on to lead his country to victory.

When we encourage others, we never know what the outcome will be, or what impact we might have.

Some of you may have read Martha Baker's syndicated column this weekend when she wrote about the value of having what she called, "guiding mothers." According to Mrs. Baker, "guiding mothers" are any older women who offer help or inspire others. She said, "They are hard to find, but a great treat to discover."

She wrote, "I just want someone older to recognize me . . . to ask about my work . . . someone happy to hug me with *arms* or *words*."

This is why these recognitions today are so important in all our lives, both for those who receive and those who give. We are both blessed.

I hope these few thoughts today will encourage you to reexamine your own dreams. I hope that on your way home—or when you get home—that you will take out your dreams and dust them off. Update them. Go to work on them again.

In doing so, you will find what Louisa May Alcott discovered to be true. She wrote, "Far away in the sunshine are my highest aspirations. I may not reach them, but I can look up and see the beauty, believe in them, and follow where they lead."

I am convinced that something happens to us in the passionate pursuit of a goal.

We are transformed.

We are made better by the attempt.

So regardless of your age or circumstances, hold on to your dreams.

Pursue them relentlessly.

Never let them go.

Never.

*"They may forget what you said,
but they will never forget how you made them feel."*
~ Carl W. Buehner

Two other books available by
Jean Carnahan

If Walls Could Talk:
The Story of Missouri's First Families

A 440-page, coffee table book with more than 600 illustrations, most in color. This intriguing history takes you inside the Missouri Governor's Mansion for a look at the families who lived there and the difficulties they faced. Well researched and packed with humorous anecdotes, this attractive volume makes a wonderful gift or addition to a home library.

Christmas at the Mansion: Its Memories and Menus

Christmas celebrations, past and present, are featured in this 145-page, colorful portrayal of the Missouri Governor's Mansion and its wonderful Victorian decorations. Includes more than 100 Mansion recipes. Menus range from fancy state dinners and afternoon teas to family Christmas dinner and everyday fare. A splendid gift book.

Order Form

If Walls Could Talk: The Story of Missouri's First Families

_____ copies @ $50 each $_____
Shipping/Handling $6 per copy $_____

Christmas at the Mansion: Its Memories and Menus

_____ copies @ $30 each $_____
Shipping/Handling $4 per copy $_____

                                   Total $_____

❑Check enclosed payable to Governor's Mansion Gift Shop
❑Charge my account: ❑VISA ❑MasterCard
Account No. _____ Exp. Date _____
Name _____
Address _____
City/State/ZIP_____
Phone_____

Mail to
Governor's Mansion Gift Shop
P. O. Box 1133
Jefferson City, MO 65102
or call toll free 877-526-8123
Fax: 573-751-9219 www.missourimansion.org